Allergies

Edward Edelson

Introduction by C. Everett Koop, M.D., Sc.D.
Former Surgeon General, U.S. Public Health Service

Foreword by Sandra Thurman
Director, Office of National AIDS Policy, The White House

CHELSEA HOUSE PUBLISHERS
Philadelphia

The goal of the 21ST CENTURY HEALTH AND WELLNESS is to provide general information in the ever-changing areas of physiology, psychology, and related medical issues. The titles in this series are not intended to take the place of the professional advice of a physician or other health-care professional.

COVER PHOTOS: Zöe the Cat and Sunflower courtesy of Sara Davis

Chelsea House Publishers
EDITOR IN CHIEF: Stephen Reginald
MANAGING EDITOR: James D. Gallagher
PRODUCTION MANAGER: Pam Loos
ART DIRECTOR: Sara Davis
DIRECTOR OF PHOTOGRAPHY: Judy Hasday
SENIOR PRODUCTION EDITOR: Lee Anne Gelletly
ASSISTANT EDITOR: Anne Hill
PRODUCTION SERVICES: Pre-Press Company, Inc.
COVER DESIGNER/ILLUSTRATOR: Keith Trego

The Chelsea House World Wide Web site address is http://www.chelseahouse.com

1 3 5 7 9 8 6 4 2

Library of Congress Cataloging in Publication Data

Edelson, Edward, 1932-
Allergies / Edward Edelson.
p.   cm. — (21st century health and wellness)
Includes bibliographical references and index.
Summary: An in-depth look at allergies, which affect one in every five Americans in some form.
ISBN 0-7910-5523-X
1. Allergy—Juvenile literature. [1. Allergy.] I. Title. II. Series.

RC585.E34 1999
616.97—dc21

99-047866

CONTENTS

24.95

21ST CENTURY HEALTH AND WELLNESS

- **AIDS**
- **Allergies**
- **The Circulatory System**
- **The Digestive System**
- **The Immune System**
- **Mononucleosis and Other Infectious Diseases**
- **Organ Transplants**
- **Pregnancy & Birth**
- **The Respiratory System**
- **Sexually Transmitted Diseases**
- **Sports Medicine**

PREVENTION AND EDUCATION: THE KEYS TO GOOD HEALTH

C. Everett Koop, M.D., Sc.D.
FORMER SURGEON GENERAL,
U.S. Public Health Service

The issue of health education has received particular attention in recent years because of the presence of AIDS in the news. But our response to this particular tragedy points up a number of broader issues that doctors, public health officials, educators, and the public face. In particular, it spotlights the importance of sound health education for citizens of all ages.

Over the past 35 years, this country has been able to achieve dramatic declines in the death rates from heart disease, stroke, accidents, and—for people under the age of 45—cancer. Today, Americans generally eat better and take better care of themselves than ever before. Thus, with the help of modern science and technology, they have a better chance of surviving serious—even catastrophic—illnesses. In 1996, the life expectancy of Americans reached an all-time high of 76.1 years. That's the good news.

The flip side of this advance has special significance for young adults. According to a report issued in 1998 by the U.S. Department of Health and Human Services, levels of wealth and education in the United States are directly correlated with our population's health. The more money Americans make and the more years of schooling they have, the better their health will be. Furthermore, income inequality increased in the U.S. between 1970 and 1996. Basically, the rich got richer—people in high income brackets had greater increases in the amount of money made than did those at low income levels. In addition, the report indicated that children under 18 are more likely to live in poverty than the population as a whole.

Family income rises with each higher level of education for both men and women from every ethnic and racial background. Life expectancy, too, is related to family income. People with lower incomes tend to die at younger ages than people from more affluent homes. What all this means is that health is a factor of wealth and education, both of which need to be improved for all Americans if the promise of life, liberty, and the pursuit of happiness is to include an equal chance for good health.

The health of young people is further threatened by violent death and injury, alcohol and drug abuse, unwanted pregnancies, and sexually transmitted diseases. Adolescents are particularly vulnerable because they are beginning to explore their own sexuality and perhaps to experiment with drugs and alcohol. We need to educate young people to avoid serious dangers to their health. The price of neglect is high.

Even for the population as a whole, health is still far from what it could be. Why? Most death and disease are attributed to four broad elements: inadequacies in the health-care system, behavioral factors or unhealthy lifestyles, environmental hazards, and human biological factors. These categories are also influenced by individual resources. For example, low birth weight and infant mortality are more common among the children of less educated mothers. Likewise, women with more education are more likely to obtain prenatal care during pregnancy. Mothers with fewer than 12 years of education are almost 10 times more likely to smoke during pregnancy—and new studies find excessive aggression later in life as well as other physical ailments among the children of smokers. In short, poor people with less education are more likely to smoke cigarettes, which endangers health and shortens the life span. About a third of the children who begin smoking will eventually have their lives cut short because of this practice.

Similarly, poor children are exposed more often to environmental lead, which causes a wide range of physical and mental problems. Sedentary lifestyles are also more common among teens with lower family income than among wealthier adolescents. Being overweight—a condition associated with physical inactivity as well as excessive caloric intake—is also more common among poor, non-Hispanic, white adolescents. Children from rich families are more likely to have health insurance. Therefore, they are more apt to receive vaccinations and other forms of early preventative medicine and treatment. The bottom line is that kids from lower income groups receive less adequate health care.

To be sure, some diseases are still beyond the control of even the most advanced medical techniques that our richest citizens can afford. Despite yearnings that are as old as the human race itself, there is no "fountain of youth" to prevent aging and death. Still, solutions are available for many of the problems that undermine sound health. In a word, that solution is prevention. Prevention, which includes health promotion and education, can save lives, improve the quality of life, and, in the long run, save money.

In the United States, organized public health activities and preventative medicine have a long history. Important milestones include the improvement of sanitary procedures and the development of pasteurized milk in the late-19th century, and the introduction in the mid-20th century of effective vaccines against polio, measles, German measles, mumps, and other once-rampant diseases. Internationally, organized public health efforts began on a wide-scale basis with the International Sanitary Conference of 1851, to which 12 nations sent representatives. The World Health Organization, founded in 1948, continues these efforts under the aegis of the United Nations, with particular emphasis on combating communicable diseases and the training of health-care workers.

Despite these accomplishments, much remains to be done in the field of prevention. For too long, we have had a medical system that is science and technology-based, and focuses essentially on illness and mortality. It is now patently obvious that both the social and the economic costs of such a system are becoming insupportable.

Implementing prevention and its corollaries, health education and health promotion, is the job of several groups of people. First, the medical and scientific professions need to continue basic scientific research, and here we are making considerable progress. But increased concern with prevention will also have a decided impact on how primary-care doctors practice medicine. With a shift to health-based rather than morbidity-based medicine, the role of the "new physician" includes a healthy dose of patient education.

Second, practitioners of the social and behavioral sciences—psychologists, economists, and city planners along with lawyers, business leaders, and government officials—must solve the practical and ethical dilemmas confronting us: poverty, crime, civil rights, literacy, education, employment, housing, sanitation, environmental protection, health-care delivery systems, and so forth. All of these issues affect public health.

Third is the public at large. We consider this group to be important in any movement. Fourth, and the linchpin in this effort, is the public health profession: doctors, epidemiologists, teachers—who must harness the professional expertise of the first two groups and the common sense and cooperation of the third: the public. They must define the problems statistically and qualitatively and then help set priorities for finding solutions.

To a very large extent, improving health statistics is the responsiblity of every individual. So let's consider more specifically what the role of the individual should be and why health education is so important. First, and most obviously, individuals can protect themselves from illness and injury and thus minimize the need for professional medical care. They can eat a nutritious diet; get adequate exercise; avoid tobacco, alcohol, and drugs; and take prudent steps to avoid accidents. The proverbial "apple a day keeps the doctor away" is not so far from the truth, after all.

Second, individuals should actively participate in their own medical care. They should schedule regular medical and dental checkups. If an illness or injury develops, they should know when to treat themselves and when to seek professional help. To gain the maximum benefit from any medical treatment, individuals must become partners in treatment. For instance, they should understand the effects and side effects of medications. I counsel young physicians that there is no such thing as too much information when talking with patients. But the corollary is the patient must know enough about the nuts and bolts of the healing process to understand what the doctor is telling him or her. That responsibility is at least partially the patient's.

Education is equally necessary for us to understand the ethical and public policy issues in health care today. Sometimes individuals will encounter these issues in making decisions about their own treatment or that of family members. Other citizens may encounter them as jurors in medical malpractice cases. But we all become involved, indirectly, when we elect our public officials, from school board members to the president. Should surrogate parenting be legal? To what extent is drug testing desirable, legal, or necessary? Should there be public funding for family planning, hospitals, various types of medical research, and medical care for the indigent? How should we allocate scant technological resources, such as kidney dialysis and organ transplants? What is the proper role of government in protecting the rights of patients?

What are the broad goals of public health in the United States today? The Public Health Service has defined these goals in terms of mortality, education, and health improvement. It identified 15 major concerns: controlling high blood pressure, improving family planning, pregnancy care and infant health, increasing the rate of immunization, controlling sexually transmitted diseases, controlling the presence of toxic agents or radiation in the environment, improving occupational safety and health, preventing accidents, promoting water fluoridation and dental health, controlling infectious diseases, decreasing smoking, decreasing alcohol and drug abuse, improving nutrition, promoting physical fitness and exercise, and controlling stress and violent behavior. Great progress has been made in many of these areas. For example, the report *Health, United States, 1998* indicates that in general, the workplace is safer today than it was a decade ago. Between 1980 and 1993, the overall death rate from occupational injuries dropped 45 percent to 4.2 deaths per 100,000 workers.

For healthy adolescents and young adults (ages 15 to 24), the specific goal defined by the Public Health Service was a 20% reduction in deaths, with a special focus on motor vehicle injuries as well as alcohol and drug abuse. For adults (ages 25 to 64), the aim was 25% fewer deaths, with a concentration on heart attacks, strokes, and cancers. In the 1999 National Drug Control Strategy, the White House Office of National Drug Control Policy echoed the Congressional goal of reducing drug use by 50 percent in the coming decade.

Smoking is perhaps the best example of how individual behavior can have a direct impact on health. Today cigarette smoking is recognized as the most important single preventable cause of death in our society. It is responsible for more cancers and more cancer deaths than any other known agent; is a prime risk factor for heart and blood vessel disease, chronic bronchitis, and emphysema; and is a frequent cause of complications in pregnancies and of babies born prematurely, underweight, or with potentially fatal respiratory and cardiovascular problems.

Since the release of the Surgeon General's first report on smoking in 1964, the proportion of adult smokers has declined substantially, from 43% in 1965 to 30.5% in 1985. The rate of cigarette smoking among adults declined from 1974 to 1995, but rates of decline were greater among the more educated. Since 1965, more than 50 million people have quit smoking. Although the rate of adult smoking has decreased, children and teenagers are smoking more. Researchers have also noted a disturbing correlation between underage smoking of cigarettes and later use of cocaine and heroin. Although there is still much work to be done if we are to become a "smoke free society," it is heartening to note that public health and public education efforts—such as warnings on cigarette packages, bans on broadcast advertising, removal of billboards advertising cigarettes, and anti-drug youth campaigns in the media—have already had significant effects.

In 1997, the first leveling off of drug use since 1992 was found in eighth graders, with marijuana use in the past month declining to 10 percent. The percentage of eighth graders who drink alcohol or smoke cigarettes also decreased slightly in 1997. In 1994 and 1995, there were more than 142,000 cocaine-related emergency-room episodes per year, the highest number ever reported since these events were tracked starting in 1978. Illegal drugs present a serious threat to Americans who use these drugs. Addiction is a chronic, relapsing disease that changes the chemistry of the brain in harmful ways. The abuse of inhalants and solvents found in legal products like hair spray, paint thinner, and industrial cleaners—called "huffing" (through the mouth) or "sniffing" (through the nose)—has come to public attention in recent years. *The National Household Survey on Drug Abuse* discovered that among youngsters ages 12 to 17, this dangerous practice doubled between 1991 and 1996 from 10.3 percent to 21 percent. An alarming large number of children died the very first time they tried inhalants, which can also cause brain damage or injure other vital organs.

Another threat to public health comes from firearm injuries. Fortunately, the number of such assaults declined between 1993 and 1996. Nevertheless, excessive violence in our culture—as depicted in the mass media—may have contributed to the random shootings at Columbine High School in Littleton, Colorado, and elsewhere. The government and private citizens are rethinking how to reduce the fascination with violence so that America can become a safer, healthier place to live.

The "smart money" is on improving health care for everyone. Only recently did we realize that the gap between the "haves" and "have-nots" had a significant health component. One more reason to invest in education is that schooling produces better health.

In 1835, Alexis de Tocqueville, a French visitor to America, wrote, "In America, the passion for physical well-being is general." Today, as then, health and fitness are front-page items. But with the greater scientific and technological resources now available to us, we are in a far stronger position to make good health care available to everyone. With the greater technological threats to us as we approach the 21st century, the need to do so is more urgent than ever before. Comprehensive information about basic biology, preventative medicine, medical and surgical treatments, and related ethical and public policy issues can help you arm yourself with adequate knowledge to be healthy throughout life.

FOREWORD

Sandra Thurman, Director, Office of National AIDS Policy, The White House

A hundred years ago, an era was marked by discovery, invention, and the infinite possibilities of progress. Nothing peaked society's curiosity more than the mysterious workings of the human body. They poked and prodded, experimented with new remedies and discarded old ones, increased longevity and reduced death rates. But not even the most enterprising minds of the day could have dreamed of the advancements that would soon become our shared reality. Could they have envisioned that we would vaccinate millions of children against polio? Ward off the annoyance of allergy season with a single pill? Or give life to a heart that had stopped keeping time?

As we stand on the brink of a new millennium, the progress made during the last hundred years is indeed staggering. And we continue to push forward every minute of every day. We now exist in a working global community, blasting through cyber-space at the speed of light, sharing knowledge and up-to-the-minute technology. We are in a unique position to benefit from the world's rich fabric of traditional healing practices while continuing to explore advances in modern medicine. In the halls of our medical schools, tomorrow's healers are learning to appreciate the complexities of our whole person. We are not only keeping people alive, we are keeping them well.

Although we deserve to rejoice in our progress, we must also remember that our health remains a complex web. Our world changes with each step forward and we are continuously faced with new threats to our well-being. The air we breathe has become polluted, the water tainted, and new killers have emerged to challenge us in ways we are just beginning to understand. AIDS, in particular, continues to tighten its grip on America's most fragile communities, and place our next generation in jeopardy.

Facing these new challenges will require us to find inventive ways to stay healthy. We already know the dangers of alcohol, smoking and drug abuse. We also understand the benefits of early detection for illnesses like cancer and heart disease, two areas where scientists have made significant in-roads to treatment. We have become a well-informed society, and with that information comes a renewed emphasis on preventative care and a sense of personal responsibility to care for both ourselves and those who need our help.

Read. Re-read. Study. Explore the amazing working machine that is the human body. Share with your friends and your families what you have learned. It is up to all of us living together as a community to care for our well-being, and to continue working for a healthier quality of life.

1

THE IMMUNE SYSTEM

A technician tests a hay fever remedy.

Allergy is the body's defense system gone wrong. It happens when the immune system, whose purpose is to defend the body against harmful invaders, unleashes a response against something that is not really harmful. The symptoms of that allergic response can range from mildly annoying to intensely bothersome to fatal. They can also lead to life-threatening cases of asthma, a condition closely related to allergies.

About 1 out of every 5 Americans—roughly 50 million of them—suffer from allergies. Over 25 million Americans have hay fever (the formal medical name of which is *allergic rhinitis*). Close to 15 million have asthma. Another 15 million have a variety of other allergic disorders.

An allergic reaction can be triggered by pollen, plant sap, dust, mold, food, animal hair, insect venom, medication, cosmetics, and many other things found in our environment, including cold air. To understand how these reactions happen, we must take a close look at the immune system and its disorders.

We said the immune system defends the body against dangerous invaders. The worst thing that can go wrong with the immune system is a breakdown of these defenses. There is a set of extremely serious conditions called immune deficiency diseases in which that kind of breakdown occurs. Some children suffer such a breakdown because they are born without important components of the immune system. Most of them die quickly; only complete isolation or other drastic medical measures can keep them alive. It is also possible to lose part of the immune defense system. The deadly disease AIDS—acquired immune deficiency syndrome—occurs when a virus cripples an important component of the immune defense system. (AIDS will be described in more detail later in this chapter.)

There are other disorders, called autoimmune diseases, in which the immune system mistakenly attacks the body's own tissue. Insulin-dependent diabetes and rheumatoid arthritis are believed to be autoimmune diseases, as are less common conditions such as myasthenia gravis, multiple sclerosis, muscular dystrophy, and systemic lupus erythematosus. Like allergies, most of these autoimmune conditions are believed to involve both an inherited factor and environmental factors.

The bad news is that nature has given roughly one in every five of us an immune system that does not work quite the way it should. The good news is that today we know more than ever before about the nature of allergy. Laboratory studies have given scientists and physicians a detailed picture of how the immune system works and what goes wrong when it malfunctions. Because we now know so much about how the body defends itself and how the defensive response is sometimes inappropriate, we can improve the defenses against true enemies as well as lessen the inappropriate reactions and treat them more effectively when they occur.

RECOGNIZING AND ATTACKING ANTIGENS

No one would last very long without an immune defense system. We live in a hostile world, full of viruses, bacteria, fungi, yeasts, parasites, and other unfriendly creatures eager to invade the body. The immune system has evolved to recognize these invaders and do something about them. What it does can seem complicated because our immune defenses have developed over millions of years to meet a number of different challenges. Many aspects of its defenses are still not completely understood. But the basic action is simple and direct. The immune system is set up to recognize and attack substances called antigens.

An antigen is a molecule that signals the presence of an invader in the body. When the immune system recognizes an antigen, it takes steps to repel the invader. It deploys two sets of weapons: defensive cells, which attack invaders directly; and antibodies, molecules made by immune cells in response to the presence of an invader.

There are several kinds of interlinked cells and tissues designed to find antigens and respond to them. Among the most important cells are lymphocytes, which are white blood cells. They have a totally different set of functions from red blood cells, which carry oxygen throughout the body. There is only one kind of red blood cell, but there are many kinds of white blood cells. They are found not only in the arteries and veins through which blood flows but also in a second set of vessels in the body, the lymphatic vessels. We can oversimplify and say that if blood is the body's oxygen supply system, the lymph in lymphatic vessels is its garbage disposal system.

The lymphocytes that give lymph its pale yellow color originate in bone marrow, the tissue found in the center of long bones. All lymphocytes start in the bone marrow as a basic sort of cell called a stem cell. What happens to them after they leave the bone marrow depends in part on where they migrate. Stem cells that migrate to the thymus, a small organ at the base of the neck, become what are called T cells. There is another kind of lymphocyte called a B cell, which matures in the bone marrow or in outlying tissues of the lymphatic system. Another kind of white blood cell, the macrophage, follows its own path of evolution.

Macrophages, B cells, and T cells can all be found in the lymph nodes, which are small nodules that occur throughout the body. There are lymph nodes at regular intervals in the lymphatic vessels. When you get a minor infection and have "swollen glands," those glands are actually lymph nodes that are swollen because they are responding to a source of infection.

What happens in such cases is that an invader such as a virus or bacterium encounters a macrophage. The macrophage gobbles it up and digests it. Then the antigens are pushed to the outer cell wall of the

The darkened areas of this microphoto-graph indicate the presence of macrophages, a type of white blood cell. Certain types of macrophages fight infection by exposing antigens that are then weakened by antibodies.

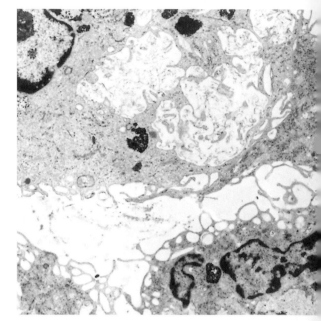

macrophage, where they are displayed in a special way that allows T cells to recognize them.

A number of different T cells respond to the display of a foreign antigen. Some are killer cells, whose function is to destroy any invading cells that have the foreign antigen. Other T cells respond by producing chemicals called lymphokines that stimulate other parts of the immune system to attack the invader. Perhaps the best-known lymphokine is interferon, which defends against viruses and cancer.

Another kind of T cell is the helper cell. One of the major roles of helper T cells is to stimulate B cells to produce antibodies. (There is another kind of T cell, the suppressor cell, which regulates antibody production by turning it off so the system is not swamped with antibodies.)

It is the T-helper cells that is the crucial victim in AIDS. Research has shown that the AIDS virus zeroes in on T-helper cells. The virus can lie dormant in them for years, or it can become active in a relatively short period of time. When the AIDS virus does become active, it kills the T-helper cells. By killing these cells, the virus cripples the immune response so severely that the body becomes vulnerable to a host of microbes that normally live within it without doing damage. The deadly

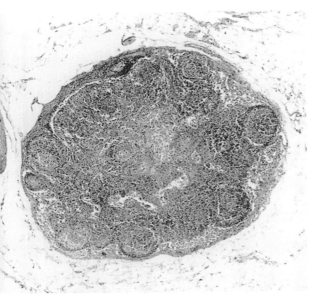

Antibodies in blood serum, magnified 32 times. Allergic responses occur when antibodies, which fight infection by destroying harmful invaders, unleash a response against something that is not really harmful.

progression of AIDS is invariably accompanied by a steady drop in T-helper cell count.

IMMUNOGLOBULINS

The lymphocytes involved in allergy are not T cells but B cells—and specifically the antibodies they produce. An antibody is a Y-shaped molecule made of long chains and short chains. Antibodies belong to a family of molecules called immunoglobulins (abbreviated Ig); *immuno-* because they are made by the immune system, *-globulin* because they have a roughly globular, round shape.

Five major classes of immunoglobulins have been identified. You have probably heard of gamma globulin (abbreviated IgG). Gamma globulin fights infection, and injections of the substance are used to fight or prevent several diseases. The immunoglobulin that allergists are concerned with is IgE. It is the one responsible for allergic reactions.

IgE has one remarkable property common to all the immunoglobulins. No matter what kind of antigen appears in the body, there will be an immunoglobulin made to match it. This ability to respond to an almost infinite number of antigens puzzled scientists for many years. Now we know that this amazing variety of antibodies is produced through adjustments in a simple basic design.

All immunoglobulins are made of two basic units, a long protein chain and a short protein chain. An IgE molecule (like other Igs) consists of two long chains and two short chains bonded together. Each short chain has what is called a hypervariable region that gives it the ability to adapt to almost any allergy-causing antigen that presents itself. This ability is enormously useful for other immunoglobulins because it allows the body to react to an enormous range of dangerous invaders.

In the case of IgE, the immunoglobulin response is less desirable. We do not know why an allergic reaction occurs, but scientists speculate that it is a now-misplaced response that originally defended the body against invasion by parasites or other enemies.

When the body of an allergy-prone person is exposed to an allergen such as ragweed pollen, B cells are stimulated to produce large amounts of IgE molecules corresponding to the specific antigen. Those IgE molecules then attach themselves to two kinds of immune system cells:

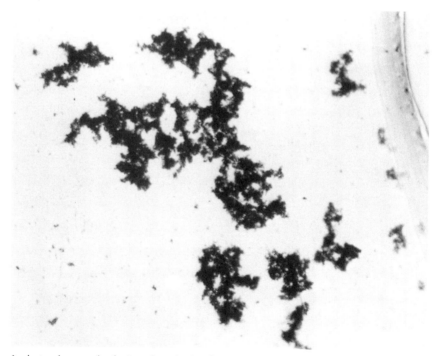

A photomicrograph of a lymph node. Swollen glands occur when these nodes, which are located throughout the human body, expand in response to the presence of an infection.

Pollens, such as the ragweed pollen collected here cause the immune system to unleash a response against them only after the organism has already been exposed and sensitized to them.

basophils, a type of white blood cell, and mast cells, which are found in tissues near small blood vessels. The immediate effect of that binding is to make both kinds of cell sensitive to the antigen. Once they are sensitized, the mast cells and basophils are ready to respond when they come in contact with the allergen again.

The immune response helps destroy dangerous invaders, such as a parasite. This service comes at the cost of irritating and painful symptoms. These symptoms are worth suffering in those instances when a danger is eliminated. They are not worth suffering if the invader poses no threat, which is the case when contact is made with an allergen.

MEDIATORS

Research has shown exactly how the contact is made between the mast cells and the basophils and the allergen and what it causes. A mast cell or basophil springs into action when an allergen binds to two IgE antibodies that have attached themselves to the cell membrane. The cell

Antihistamines and other over-the-counter remedies can provide temporary relief for some allergy symptoms, but researchers have yet to discover a medication that can quell all allergic responses.

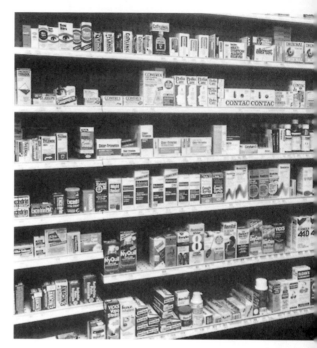

then releases a number of chemicals called mediators, which are responsible for the symptoms of an allergic reaction—the runny nose of hay fever, the itching of poison ivy, and so on. In really severe cases, the allergic response caused by mediators can be life-threatening. The most severe reaction is anaphylactic shock, which can cause death in minutes.

The best-known mediator is histamine, which was discovered in the 1920s. Its discovery led to the use of antihistamines, drugs that relieve allergy symptoms by blocking histamine activity. But we know that antihistamines give only partial relief; they do not block other mediators, which are responsible for some symptoms.

Those other mediators include a family of compounds called kinins, which are released at the same time as histamine. A little later, mast cells release a number of other mediators—prostaglandins, leukotrienes, bradykinin, and more. Most of these mediators were discovered fairly recently, and research has yet to develop effective drugs to block their activity. We will return to them later when we discuss the frontiers of allergy and immunology research.

As we have said, the immediate effect of mediator release is to cause all the annoying—and sometimes deadly—symptoms of an allergy. There can also be long-term effects that are related to the development of asthma.

We have mentioned asthma as a condition that is closely related to allergy. Some of the symptoms are the same. In an asthma attack, as in an allergic reaction, the patient can have trouble breathing because there is a tightening of the bronchi, the airways leading to the lung. That tightening is caused by mediators, one of whose effects is to cause contraction of

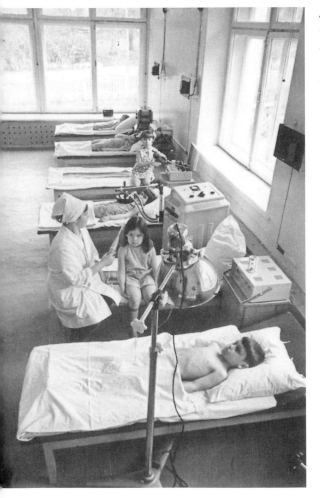

A nurse tends to an asthmatic child in a Russian sanatorium. Asthma attacks resemble certain allergic reactions in which victims suffer a tightening of the bronchi that makes breathing difficult.

the smooth muscle of the bronchi. But not all asthma is caused by an allergic response. In fact, one of every three cases of asthma has another cause. What can happen in an allergic reaction is that mediators such as histamine attract other defensive cells to the site of the allergic reaction. Those cells cause inflammation of the area; if the inflammation occurs in the bronchi, it makes the patient more vulnerable to asthmatic attacks.

You can see from this brief description that allergy is no simple matter. It involves a seemingly endless number of cell types and molecules. This complexity may seem a hindrance to researchers but in many ways it helps them in their efforts to prevent allergy or treat it better. Every link in the chain—from antigen to T cell to B cell to immunoglobulins and mediators—gives science another point of attack. We have already mentioned one successful type of treatment, the use of antihistamines to block one kind of mediator. We will talk about others as we discuss various sorts of allergy and their treatments. Right now, we will take a closer look at asthma, how it is related to allergy, and what physicians are doing to treat it.

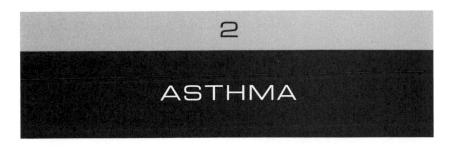

2

ASTHMA

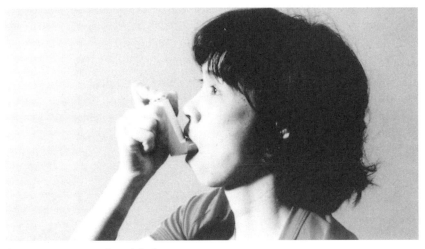

A woman uses an asthma inhaler.

Asthma was identified as a major disease more than a century ago, but it remains something of a mystery. Its name comes from the Greek word for "panting," or breathlessness, which describes one of its major symptoms. Someone with asthma experiences a tightness of the chest and labored breathing that leads to gasping, wheezing, and, in many cases, coughing. An asthma attack leaves a patient literally gasping for air.

The underlying cause of these symptoms is an unexplained sensitivity of the breathing system in asthmatics. For some unknown reason, the muscles that line an asthmatic's bronchi, the tubes that carry air to the lungs, are susceptible to spasms that make the bronchi contract, narrowing the air passages. The mucosa, the tissue that lines the air passages, is also easily inflamed, which causes further narrowing. And the cells that produce mucus to lubricate the bronchi are overactive, which also decreases air flow.

Asthma can be fatal. More than 5,000 Americans die of it every year, and, for reasons that are not known, the number of deaths have recently increased. Doctors also do not know what causes asthma. Many hypothesize, however, that it is a combination of genetic predisposition and environmental factors. There is a close parallel to allergy in that asthma also seems to be a defensive response gone wrong. It is an appropriate defense for the airways to contract when exposed to a major irritant such as smoke or dust. That contraction keeps the irritant out of the lungs. In asthma, the airways are abnormally sensitive to such irritants, but they also can react when exposed to some normally harmless substances, such as cold air.

The nature of the relationship between allergy and asthma is not entirely clear, but in many patients the two go together. Doctors often draw a distinction between "extrinsic" and "intrinsic" asthma. Extrinsic asthma most often occurs in young patients, and allergic reactions appear to be the major cause of their breathing problems. Intrinsic asthma is more often found in older patients, and it has no clear link to allergy—or indeed, to any specific cause; it can be set off by a variety of causes, including infections. Some patients, who do not fit clearly into either of the two groups, are said to have mixed asthma.

Each asthma patient must be evaluated as an individual. One patient's attacks, obviously caused by exposure to an allergen such as dog hair, can be prevented by getting the pet out of the house. Another patient may have attacks that come unpredictably, set off by psychological stress or a respiratory infection. It can also be caused by an overabundance of mediators. Some young asthma patients experience steady improvement as they grow older; in others, the disease gets steadily worse and attacks are more frequent and more intense. Psychological factors can also trigger an asthma attack, although it is important to note that the disease is not "all in the head." It is, rather, a physical disease that can have a psychological component.

DIAGNOSIS

When diagnosing asthma, it is necessary to rule out other diseases that can cause the same symptoms, including chronic bronchitis and emphysema. The doctor will start by taking a family history. Asthma is

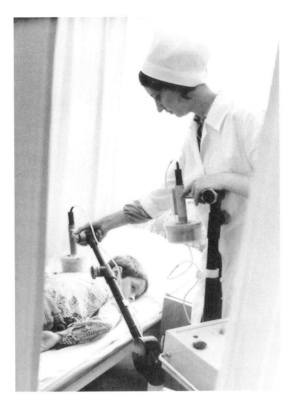

At a Moscow hospital, a nurse treats a patient who has bronchial asthma. Many doctors hypothesize that asthma results from a combination of genetic and environmental causes.

more common in people from families in which there is a history of asthma or allergy, but such a history is only an indicator. In most cases, the physician will administer a battery of tests before diagnosing asthma. It is common to test lung function, measure blood gases, and test blood for the presence of excess numbers of eosinophils, cells that are associated with asthma. It is also common to perform a challenge test, letting the patient breathe in small amounts of a substance to see if it causes asthma symptoms.

Most often, the challenge test will use methacholine, a close chemical relative of a substance known to trigger bronchial spasms, although histamine is sometimes used. Large amounts of methacholine cause the bronchi to contract in everyone; a reaction to small amounts that do not bother most people indicates asthma. Or, if the doctor suspects a specific irritant is responsible, the patient may be challenged with that substance—for example, an industrial chemical that a worker is exposed to on the job.

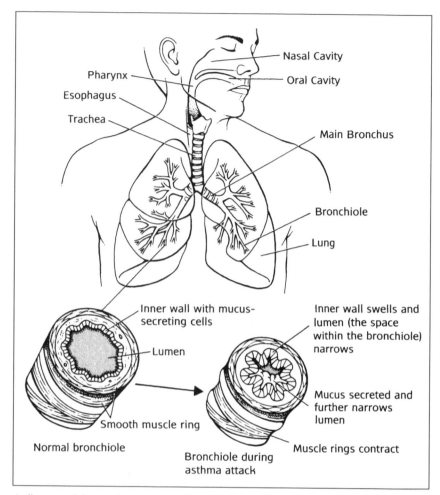

Nasal Cavity

Oral Cavity

Pharynx

Esophagus

Trachea

Main Bronchus

Bronchiole

Lung

Inner wall with mucus-secreting cells

Inner wall swells and lumen (the space within the bronchiole) narrows

Lumen

Mucus secreted and further narrows lumen

Smooth muscle ring

Muscle rings contract

Normal bronchiole

Bronchiole during asthma attack

A diagram of the respiratory system illustrates the physical changes that take place in the bronchioles during an asthma attack.

LEARNING TO COPE

The list of substances that can cause asthma attacks is long. It includes a large number of allergens, such as pollen, animal hair, house dust, some foods, and molds and fungi. Aspirin can cause or worsen an asthma attack in some patients. So can sulfites, which are used as food preservatives; there are cases in which sulfite-caused asthma attacks have been fatal. Exercise can also cause an asthma attack (especially in young patients), as can cold air or changes in the weather, tobacco smoke, and other common irritants in the air we breathe. And psychological stress can trigger an actual physical response.

The challenge of asthma to both doctor and patient is that it is a chronic disease that at present cannot be cured. But it can be managed well enough for a patient to lead a normal life. If an allergy is involved, it is vital to identify the substance or substances causing the patient's allergy. (We will discuss allergy tests in detail in the next chapter.) After the asthma-causing allergens are identified, they should be avoided as much as possible. As a rule, asthma patients should keep their homes as free as possible of dust, molds, and other allergens. They should check such things as the stuffing of furniture and bedding, the materials their curtains are made of, plants in the house, carpets and rugs, heating and air-conditioning systems, and, of course, any pets.

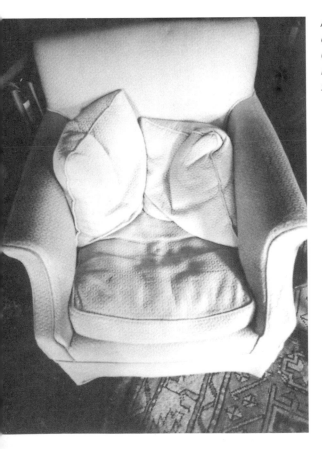

Asthma patients should keep their homes as free as possible of dust, molds, and other allergens, which often accumulate in unsuspected places, such as furniture stuffing.

One of the most serious problems for younger asthma patients is that exercise can trigger attacks. Anyone will start gasping for breath after strenuous exercise. With asthmatics, shortness of breath and wheezing begin often in exaggerated form, after only a few minutes of exercise. Asthmatics' problems with exercise are worsened if, as is often true, they are also sensitive to cold or to very dry or very humid air. And it is a double-barreled problem because asthma is easier to live with if the patient is in good physical shape; the respiratory system of someone who leads a sedentary life does not work as efficiently as it should, so air flow is not optimum.

The solution to this problem is a carefully controlled regimen of exercise, combined with drug treatment to keep asthma symptoms to a minimum. Young athletes are advised to choose sports that cause the fewest problems for them. High-endurance sports such as distance running should be avoided. Among individual sports, swimming is about the best, in part because some exposure to the humidity of a pool or lake helps reduce symptoms temporarily. Among team sports, baseball is often recommended, because it is a slower game than soccer or basketball. Brisk walking is another beneficial exercise, especially for older patients. Conditioning sessions, in which the patient works out (under the supervision of a physical therapist, if necessary), and long warmups are recommended to get the body and respiratory system into shape.

DRUG REMEDIES

Most asthma patients reduce the risk of an attack before they exercise by taking medication. Several classes of drugs are used to treat and prevent asthma attacks. They can be given orally, by aerosol spray, or by injection, and they can be prescribed singly or in combination, depending on the patient's needs. Because asthma and allergy are related, many of the same drugs are used to treat both conditions.

The largest general group of drugs used to treat asthma is composed of bronchodilators, which are drugs that expand the bronchi. The oldest family of bronchodilators is the methylxanthines. Caffeine belongs to this drug family, but the methylxanthine most widely used in asthma is called theophylline. Several chemical relatives of theophylline are also used, but they are all converted to theophylline in the body. Theo-

Swimming is probably the best form of exercise for people with bronchial asthma be-cause their symptoms can be temporarily relieved by the humidity of a lake or pool.

phylline and its cousins are available in tablet and liquid form and can be injected when a severe attack occurs.

The methylxanthines work by relaxing the muscles that line the bronchi and by improving the function of the diaphragm, which expands and contracts to draw air into the lungs. They also clear mucus from the bronchi and may reduce the release of mediators from mast cells. As with almost any drug, there is a price to be paid in the form of side effects, which can include nervousness, headaches, nausea, vomiting, and loss of appetite.

Theophylline and its relatives used to be the primary drug treatment for asthma. They have been replaced in that role, however, by a group of bronchodilators called beta-adrenergic agents or adrenergic agonists, so called because they act on adrenergic receptors, which help control breathing. A major reason for the growing use of beta-adrenergic agents is that methylxanthines have a narrow margin of safety. Side effects caused by overdoses are less likely with beta-adrenergic agents. They can be taken in pill form or as aerosol inhalants. One of the most widely used adrenergic agonists is epinephrine, which is better known

Asthma sufferer Bob Gibson starred for the St Louis Cardinals from 1959 until 1973. Baseball is recommended as an activity for asthma sufferers because it is played at a slower pace than most other team sports.

by a common brand name, Adrenalin. A number of synthetic versions of epinephrine are also available.

There are several classes of beta-adrenergic drugs, which have different effects. For example, epinephrine is a member of the family called the catecholamines. These drugs achieve peak activity just a few minutes after they are taken, but their effect wears off within two hours. By contrast, other beta-adrenergic drugs do not start working at full power for 10 to 15 minutes but can continue to relax the bronchi for as long as 6 hours. The longer-lasting beta-adrenergic drugs in common use include metproterenol and terbutaline. Asthma patients are told to take these drugs on a daily basis to help prevent attacks at the first signs of shortness of breath or wheezing and to take extra doses via a nebulizer (an atomizer that produces a fine spray for deep penetration of the lungs). One drug used entirely to prevent attacks is cromolyn sodium (its brand name is Intal), which acts by preventing the release of histamine from mast cells. Cromolyn sodium is often taken a few minutes before exercise to reduce the risk of an attack.

The most powerful drugs used to treat asthma and allergies are the corticosteroids. These are synthetic versions of hormones produced by the adrenal glands, or of hormones that stimulate the adrenal glands to secrete their hormones. The problem with the corticosteroids is that their powerful effects on asthma and allergy can be accompanied by extremely powerful adverse side effects. A list of the potential side effects of steroids could run for pages. Prolonged use of steroids can cause thinning of the skin, high blood pressure, cataracts, an increased risk of infection, ulcers, weakening of the bones, potassium deficiency, and psychological problems including depression, irritability, and even psychosis. Small wonder that wise physicians and patients use steroids as little as possible and then with great care.

One way to reduce side effects is to give steroids in aerosol form, thus maximizing their ability to open airways while minimizing the amount that is absorbed into the bloodstream to affect the rest of the body. Often, however, steroids are given orally, especially when asthma cannot be handled by any other means. In severe cases of asthma, the patient may be given high doses of steroids for two or three weeks. If continuing steroid therapy is needed, side effects can be reduced by giving the drug every other day, in small doses. Steroids sometimes are used together with aerosol bronchodilators to give more relief with fewer side effects. It is important to note that fear of steroids can be taken too far. Patients and doctors are sometimes so worried about steroid side effects that they do not use the drugs, even in emergencies.

Another drug sometimes used in aerosol form to treat asthma is atropine, but its use is limited because of side effects that include rapid heartbeat, insomnia, blurred vision, and dry mouth. Ipratropium is a drug that acts in the same way as atropine but has fewer side effects. Antihistamines can be prescribed to relieve some symptoms of asthma; antibiotics can be used to reduce the risk of respiratory infections that often accompany asthma. The exact combination of drugs and the timing of their use must be tailored for each patient.

The worst danger for asthmatics is a life-threatening condition called status asthmaticus, a severe attack that does not respond to conventional treatment. It calls for hospitalization, as do other truly severe asthma attacks. Major medical centers have respiratory intensive care units equipped for continuous monitoring that includes frequent blood testing, as well as intravenous injections of steroids and other drugs if required.

Fortunately, the vast majority of asthma patients never need that kind of emergency care. By taking good care of themselves, using drugs when needed, and avoiding the things that trigger attacks, most patients can live a normal life. As we have mentioned, the factor that causes symptoms in asthma is an allergic reaction. Let us now look at how doctors track down the presence of an allergy and identify specific allergens.

3

ALLERGY TESTS
AND ALLERGENS

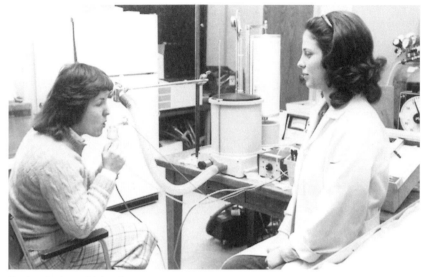

Testing for bronchial asthma.

Many people who have allergies do not realize it. They go through life complaining about a succession of colds that seem to plague them for no reason. The symptoms of a cold and of allergic rhinitis—hay fever—are almost identical: sneezing, stuffiness, a running nose, itching throat, weepy eyes. Allergy should be suspected when the symptoms do not go away, when they recur regularly (during the summer pollen season, for example), or when there are other symptoms of allergy: skin rashes, stomach and bowel problems such as persistent indigestion and abdominal pain, or breathing problems such as wheezing and shortness of breath.

A family history and physical examination often provide enough information for a doctor to diagnose the presence of an allergy. Simple questioning can give good clues to the cause of an allergic reaction: for example, if the symptoms began when the family bought a pet, or if they occur during the ragweed pollen season. But often, some tests are needed.

ALLERGY TESTS

Skin Tests

The doctor may perform a skin test, in which the patient is exposed to an extract of the suspected allergen. Other methods include a scratch test, in which the suspected allergen is applied directly to small scratches in the skin, and a prick test, in which the skin is pricked with a needle after the extract is applied. The doctor waits for about 20 minutes and looks for a wheel, a small, circular area of itching, reddening, and swelling that is a sign of an allergic reaction. But a positive reaction on a skin test just means that someone has antibodies to that allergen. It does not mean that the allergen will cause symptoms. The results of a skin test have to be correlated with the patient's actual experience when exposed to the allergen.

RAST

When a skin test cannot be done (for example, if the patient has a skin condition), the doctor may perform a RAST, or radioallergosorbent test. The RAST test is no more sensitive than a skin test and costs a lot more, but it does not require the patient to be exposed to the allergen. A sample of blood is sent to a laboratory where it is exposed to radioactively tagged allergens. A radiation detection device then is used to detect whether the blood has antibodies to the allergen.

If the suspected allergen is a food, the doctor often prescribes an elimination challenge diet. The patient is first told to limit the diet to a small number of foods that usually do not cause allergic reactions. Then the suspected foods are added to the diet, one at a time, while the patient is watched for an allergic reaction. Because it takes so much time and requires a great deal of discipline, an elimination diet is best when there is only a small list of suspected foods.

Blood Tests

In a few cases, the doctor may do a blood test to confirm the presence of allergies, looking for high concentrations of eosinophils, white blood cells that take part in the allergic response, or of IgE. Blood tests are not always accurate, but they can help lead to a diagnosis.

CLINICAL ECOLOGISTS

There is yet another set of tests that are the subjects of even greater doubt—not only about the tests themselves but also about the unusual allergies they purport to detect. These tests are given by practitioners who may call themselves "clinical ecologists" or "otolaryngic [involving the ear, nose, and throat] allergists." In general, their approach is the same. They believe that a large number of substances—foods and chemicals in our environment—can trigger subtle allergic reactions. These reactions are said to cause a long list of vague complaints that include depression, fatigue, minor aches and pain, headaches, general malaise, and other, often mysterious illnesses.

Generally, these practitioners make a diagnosis by performing their own kind of challenge test. In one such test, a food extract is injected under the skin. Instead of looking for an allergic skin reaction, the practitioner looks for such symptoms as discomfort, fever, and drowsiness. In another such test, the same symptoms are supposed to occur when the same food extract is placed under the tongue. Those extracts often are used to treat the purported allergy.

The claims made by these practitioners have never been verified by carefully controlled scientific studies. Their challenge tests and extract treatments have been described as having "no plausible rationale or immunologic basis" by the American Academy of Allergy and Immunology, and an expert committee of the federal Food and Drug Administration has said that food extract treatments are ineffective.

IMMUNOTHERAPY

Injections are controversial even in mainstream allergy treatment. The concept behind them is simple and sound: to prevent allergic reactions by exposing the patient to small amounts of an allergen over a long period of time, thus making the immune system less sensitive. Allergy injections—formally called immunotherapy—are controversial because some allergists feel they are overused and because of questions about the quality of the extracts used in the treatment.

Money is one reason for the controversy. A patient who accepts immunotherapy must take a series of injections for months or years. The doctor who gives them gets a fee for each injection. In general, allergists say injections should be regarded as a last line of defense, to be used when other methods have not given adequate relief. The best way to prevent an allergic response is by avoiding the allergen; if you are allergic to cats, do not have one in the house; if you are allergic to ragweed pollen, go to a ragweed-free area during the hay fever season. When avoidance is impossible, the next line of defense is drug treatment. If that does not work, if the symptoms are serious enough to interfere with normal life, and if the cause of the reaction is clearly identified, immunotherapy can help.

Injections generally are used for allergies to pollen, molds, insect venom, and house dust—not for foods, where avoidance is the simplest and most effective measure. The extracts are prepared by grinding the material, dissolving the allergen in liquid, straining it out of the liquid and then sterilizing it. What allergists would like from this process is a standardized set product that would give predictable results when injected into any patient.

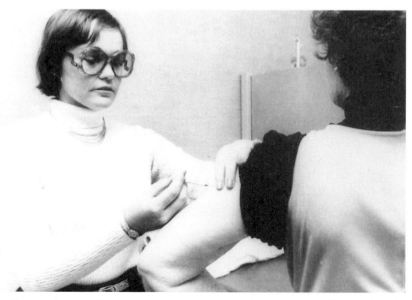

A patient receives an allergy shot or—in medical terms—immunotherapy. This treatment prevents allergic reactions by exposing the patient to small amounts of an allergen over long periods of time.

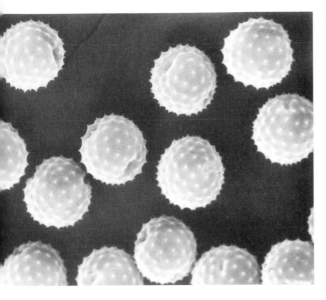

A major irritant for many allergy suffer-ers is ragweed pollen, magnified here 8,000 times. Immunotherapy has proved an effective treatment, but doctors prefer to use it only as a last resort.

Although standardization has not been achieved for most extracts (more than 1,000 are available), there are standard products for the most important allergens, such as ragweed pollen, some grass pollens, cat hair, and the mites often found in house dust.

These extracts are available in different strengths. The weakest are given once a week or once every two weeks when the treatment begins. Weak doses are given because of the risk that the extracts can cause allergic reactions. The most common side effect is a local reaction at the site of the injection—essentially the same kind of itching, swelling, and redness seen in a skin test. But there is a small possibility of a danger-ous reaction called anaphylaxis, which is a violent allergic response affecting the entire body. Anaphylaxis usually begins only a few minutes after the shot is given. It causes an exaggerated set of allergic symptoms (weepy eyes, nasal blockage, reddened skin), which can be accompanied by breathing difficulties, a drop in blood pressure, and other problems that, in the most serious cases, can be life threatening. The doctor should monitor the patient carefully for such symptoms.

If no adverse reactions occur, stronger injections of the extracts are given, often weekly, until a long-term maintenance level is reached—possibly in a few months, possibly after a year or so. The time between injections is then lengthened, until the shots are given once a month. Improvement should occur after a year. If there is no improvement after two years, immunotherapy should be discontinued. In any event, it should be stopped after three to five years. Perhaps half of all patients will have permanent relief. If allergy symptoms come back, immunotherapy can be started again.

Studies of the effectiveness of immunotherapy for specific allergies have produced varying results. Injections have been shown to be effective for people who suffer serious allergic reactions from insect stings, pollens, and animal dander. They are usually not recommended for food allergies. Work to produce more effective extracts has been underway since the 1960s. The most promising extracts use what are called polymerized allergens, in which several allergens are linked together by a chemical process. Several studies indicate that polymerized allergens are effective with many fewer shots than existing products and also cause fewer side effects. They have not yet been approved for general use.

It is not entirely clear yet how immunotherapy works, but research has given some important clues. Its main effect apparently is to induce production of blocking antibodies that prevent allergens from interacting with mast cells and basophils, the cells that release the mediators that cause allergy symptoms. Immunotherapy also seems to reduce production of IgE antibodies and to increase the activity of T-suppressor cells, but the contribution of its effects to symptom relief has not been established.

It was stated earlier that immunotherapy should be used only after other treatments fail. As noted in the previous chapter, many asthma drugs are also used to treat allergies. Steroids, for example, are used to treat both conditions. They can be taken orally, as a nasal spray, or as a cream or ointment for skin allergies. The bronchodilators prescribed for asthma are also used against allergies. One major difference is that antihistamines, which play a relatively small role in asthma treatment, are used commonly to treat allergies. We will describe specific drug therapy in discussions of the major types of allergy, beginning with the most common kind, hay fever.

4

HAY FEVER

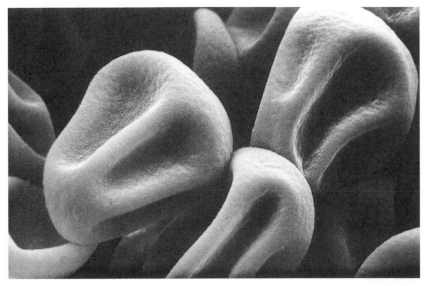

Grass pollen, magnified 6,000 times.

By this time it may be clear that *hay fever* is a misnomer. In fact, no one is allergic to hay. But millions of Americans—more than 40 million, to be exact—are allergic to pollens, most often to ragweed pollen. A pollen allergy that occurs during the ragweed season, which runs from August into October, is called hay fever. If the allergic symptoms occur in the spring, they are likely to be called rose fever—another mistaken name; allergic reactions to flower pollen are very rare. Most flower pollens are so heavy they do not float in the air, where they might get into sensitive nasal passages. Even if one is allergy prone, one would have to bury one's face in a bouquet of flowers and sniff hard to suffer a reaction to flower pollen.

A golfer demonstrates one way to relieve hay fever symptoms. The season for pollen allergies—allergic rhinitis— usually begins in spring and lasts until the first autumn frost.

POLLEN ALLERGIES

The medical name for hay fever and other pollen allergies is *allergic rhinitis* (the word *rhinitis is* derived from a Greek word meaning the nose; thus the term signifies that the problem occurs in the nose). Many substances other than pollens can cause allergic rhinitis, but pollens are the chief villains. Typically, in most parts of the United States an allergist's telephone starts ringing in springtime, when trees start shedding their pollen. The season runs to the first frost of autumn.

Each region of the country has its own contributors to the problem and its own schedule. For example, in the Northeast the season begins about April 1, when maple trees start shedding pollen. They are followed by willows, oaks, birches, and others for four to six weeks, when trees finish their pollinating cycle. In central and southern California, the tree-pollen season runs from January through the end of May. Farther north on the West Coast, tree pollen is in the air from early January to June. Even Alaska has a brief tree-pollen season in the spring.

The tree-pollen season overlaps with that of grasses, which in the Northeast generally begins at the end of April and runs through the beginning of July. Then there is a brief pause, until ragweed plants start shedding their pollen to provide a grand finale. (Some allergy patients do not get the benefit of that pause. They are allergic to the spores that molds send into the air all through the spring and summer.) But it should be emphasized that this schedule just applies to the Northeast. Someone who lives in Florida may suffer in January, when oak, cypress, and maple pollens are in the air. An allergist will have a detailed schedule of which pollens are in the air at specific times of the year for the region in which he or she practices.

Pollen Counts

Many hospitals mark the beginning of the allergic rhinitis season by taking pollen counts. A pollen count is supposed to tell allergy sufferers how bad the problem is on any given day, but it is not totally reliable, partly because a pollen count applies to the location where it is made; wind patterns or other factors may make the situation completely different only a short distance away.

A pollen count may also be difficult to interpret because two different systems are in use. The basic method is the same. A sticky slide is exposed to the air for a set time period, then the number of pollen grains on the slide is counted. An older method uses a stationary slide. A newer technique is to spin the slide. The newer method, which is rapidly replacing the old, gives much higher pollen counts and is regarded as more accurate. The numbers tell which method is being used. If the pollen count is in the teens, it was probably taken with a stationary slide. A count in the hundreds means a revolving slide was used. Under the new system a pollen count less than 100 is low, up to 500 is moderate, between 500 and 1,000 is high, and more than 1,000 is terrible.

DUST, MITE, AND MOLD ALLERGIES

Pollen allergies can be worsened if the patient is exposed at the same time to other allergens, such as pet hair or house dust. The latter is one of the most common allergens, and one that is often overlooked. House dust has a number of ingredients: tiny fibers from furniture, animal dander, microscopic bits of human skin, food remnants, detergent fragments, and more. In recent years, allergists have focused attention on house-dust mites, insects too small to be seen by the naked eye.

These mites are relatives of ticks and spiders and are classified as belonging to the genus *Dermatophagoides.* They can live almost anywhere in the house and are found in greatest numbers in beds, furniture, and rugs. Fragments of the mites themselves can be allergens, as can substances found in their droppings. A thorough housecleaning to reduce the amount of dust and the number of mites is essential for anyone with house-dust allergy.

Doctors will suspect house-dust allergy if the patient suffers year-round symptoms that flare up during spring cleaning or at other times when the amount of dust in the air is increased. Among the measures recommended is thoroughly cleaning mattresses, box springs, and pillows, which should then be put in dust-proof covers. Carpets should be removed from the bedroom of the allergy sufferer. Floors (and the rest of the room) should be cleaned at least once a week. Humidity should be kept low, because house mites flourish only when the humidity is more than 20%. Overstuffed and ornate furniture should be kept out of the allergic person's room because it traps so much dust. Pets, furs, stuffed animals, and other potential sources of allergens should also be banished from the person's room.

Cleaning the house to get rid of molds requires other steps. Molds grow readily in the warm, damp atmosphere of bathrooms; these should be kept well ventilated and cleaned thoroughly, with a fungicide

Grains of pollen clinging to a hemlock tree are magnified 60 times their normal size at top left, 500 times at top right, 1,700 times at lower left, and 8,000 times at lower right.

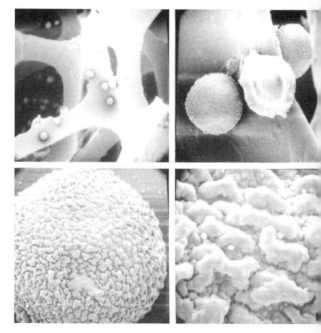

if necessary. Damp basements can also be breeding grounds for molds; a dehumidifier can reduce their growth. Pillows are another potential source of molds and should be replaced every year or two. Foods can also contain molds, a phenomenon that will be explored in the chapter on food allergies.

Air conditioners can have both good and bad effects on allergy patients. If air conditioner filters are not cleaned or replaced regularly, they can collect molds and pollens. But if air conditioners are kept in the recirculating mode so they do not draw in air from outside and if their filters are kept clean, they can reduce the amount of allergens in the air appreciably.

Electronic air-filtering machines are even more effective. These sophisticated devices, based on space-program technology, can remove as much as 99% of airborne pollutants. The most effective are so-called HEPA, or high-energy particulate-arresting, filters. These tend to be expensive, costing about as much as an air conditioner. Some machines combine HEPA and charcoal filters for even greater efficiency.

Other steps that can be taken to make a house allergy-proof include banning smoking and pets. But even if all these measures are taken, the problem of allergic rhinitis remains difficult to combat. No one can prevent trees, grasses, and ragweed from releasing pollen. For someone who has the time and the money, the best treatment is a trip to a pollen-free area. An ocean cruise is most effective because it takes the allergy sufferer many miles from all pollens. If the allergy can be traced to a specific pollen, such as ragweed, a trip to the mountains, where little or no ragweed grows, or to other low-ragweed areas usually works. Patients are warned, however, to check the pollen levels of a vacation spot in advance. Some parts of the Southwest, once known as a pollen-free haven for allergy sufferers, are not recommended now because population growth has brought both a heavy increase in air pollution and high concentrations of pollen from the trees and plants of new residents.

MEDICAL MEASURES

For the great majority of allergy sufferers who cannot travel, treatment usually starts with an antihistamine. There are many choices available, because the antihistamines now on the market are members of six chemical families that act in different ways to achieve the same goal, reduction of histamine activity. If the symptoms are minor, an over-the-counter antihistamine such as Benadryl or Chlor-Trimeton (both of which were once prescription drugs) might be enough to bring relief. Otherwise, the doctor will try one prescription or another product to find one that gives relief with the fewest side effects. The major side effect of antihistamines is drowsiness, which can be serious enough to interfere with work, driving, and other activities. Some anti-histamines cause less drowsiness than others, but until recently none was completely free of the effect. Now there are several prescription an-tihistamines that do not cause drowsiness.

Antihistamines are often given in combination with deconges-tants, which help prevent runny noses. Decongestants can be taken orally or as a nasal spray. The most widely used oral decongestants

Low-ragweed areas, such as mountains, are ideal for vacationers who are allergic to ragweed pollen. Such sufferers should find out in advance if much ragweed grows near a vacation spot.

Some over-the-counter medications can relieve minor hay fever symptoms. If these remedies do not help, a patient may try a prescription decongestant or, as a last resort, immunotherapy.

are pseudoephedrine (whose brand names include Novafed and Sudafed), phenylephrine, and phenylpropanolamine. Nasal spray decongestants include phenylephrine (whose brand names include Neo-Synephrine, Allerest, and Coricidin), tetrahydrozoline, naphazoline, and oxymetazoline.

Decongestants have their own set of side effects, including nervousness, dizziness, and nausea. Nasal spray decongestants have another side effect that can sneak up on a user. If taken for too long, nasal decongestants can cause a rebound effect, increasing symptoms rather than decreasing them. People can start taking larger and more frequent doses in a vicious cycle that can lead to chronic inflammation of nasal tissue. It is even possible to become addicted to a nasal spray decongestant, which is good reason for taking them only for relatively brief periods (perhaps a week or so).

If an antihistamine-decongestant combination does not provide relief, the next step will probably be a prescription for a corticosteroid nasal spray. A nasal spray of this drug is preferred over the oral form for allergic rhinitis because it has fewer side effects; the medication goes directly to the site of the problem, the nose, not to the rest of the body. Corticosteroid eyedrops may be prescribed to relieve allergy-caused eye irritation.

Another drug used to treat allergic rhinitis is cromolyn sodium (brand name Intal). It is taken on a regular schedule, not to treat symptoms but to prevent them. Some asthma patients use an inhalant to deliver cromolyn through the mouth to prevent attacks. Allergy sufferers may take it as a nasal spray, often along with an antihistamine-decongestant combination. Cromolyn is also available in eyedrop form.

As mentioned earlier, immunotherapy—allergy injections—can ease symptoms for those who can accept the discipline and expense of the treatment. Immunotherapy can be highly effective against allergic reactions to insect stings, pollens, and animal dander. It is generally not recommended for treatment of food allergies, however.

Allergy shots can bring long-lasting relief of symptoms for patients who are not helped by drug treatment. The usual schedule for pollen immunotherapy is one shot a week for at least a year, then shots every two or four weeks for another two to four years. If there is no improvement after the first year, the shots should be stopped. Allergists report good to excellent results, often lasting after the shots have been discontinued, in about 80% of patients with pollen allergies.

Allergic rhinitis usually starts in childhood or the teen years. But it can develop at almost any age, although it rarely begins after 50. But it should be noted that sufferers of hay fever and other forms of allergic rhinitis often get better with age. Sometimes allergy symptoms diminish markedly in middle age, and for no apparent reason. Symptoms usually reach a peak in the early 30s for men, in the late 30s for women. So allergy sufferers can hope for one small benefit of getting older.

5

FOOD ALLERGIES

Wheat, a common allergen.

Food allergies are a source of immense confusion and controversy. Some idea of the confusion can be gleaned from a list of definitions issued by the American Academy of Allergy and Immunology, which distinguishes among such terms as adverse food reaction, food idiosyncrasy, food sensitivity, and food hypersensitivity (only the last term means a true food allergy, according to the academy). The controversy centers on claims that allergies to foods or food additives can cause a number of physical, psychological, and mental problems, such as learning disabilities in children.

MILD TO FATAL REACTIONS

Food allergy symptoms can occur all through the body, ranging from a mild bellyache to sudden death. If we follow the path food takes as it is eaten, we would expect the first signs of an allergic reaction to occur at the lips, mouth and throat, in the form of swelling and itching. If an allergic reaction occurs when the food moves into the stomach and then the intestines, the symptoms can include nausea, vomiting, bowel cramps, diarrhea, and migraine headaches. Food allergy can also affect other parts of the body. The reaction can occur in the respiratory system, causing asthma attacks and breathing problems, sometimes serious enough to cause death by suffocation. Skin symptoms can also occur. The most common is hives, patches of reddening, itching, and swelling. Another skin reaction, atopic dermatitis, is the subject of controversy. Most allergists believe food allergens can cause or worsen atopic dermatitis, which is characterized by itchy skin and inflammation. Others say a link has not been proved. Recent studies have shown that food allergens can make the symptoms worse in some patients.

The greatest danger of food allergens comes from anaphylaxis, a violent allergic reaction that occurs throughout the body. Anaphylactic shock, as it is also called, causes severe nausea, vomiting, swelling, chest pain, choking, and collapse. Unless immediate treatment is given, anaphylaxis can be fatal. People have died from eating a single peanut or another food that caused an anaphylactic reaction. Anaphylaxis can also be caused by nonfood allergens, such as medications and insect venoms. (First aid for anaphylaxis will be discussed later.)

The most controversial reactions that have been associated with food allergies are those purported to affect psychological or mental performance. In Chapter 3, we mentioned the methods used by "clinical ecologists," who link food allergies to a wide range of ill-defined disorders. Some researchers have made similar claims about possible links between food allergies and childhood problems including hyperactivity—an inability to sit still and concentrate—and learning disabilities such as dyslexia, which is the inability to read properly despite normal intelligence.

Dietary substances that are alleged to be linked to these problems include salicylate (the active ingredient in aspirin; it is also found in some meats, starches, fruits, vegetables, and other foods), artificial colorings and other food additives, and sugar. Most scientifically controlled studies have not been able to verify these allegations, although researchers have found indications that a small percentage of children may experience minor but measurable reactions to some of the suspect food products. At the present time, most experts do not believe that food allergies are a major cause of behavior or learning problems in children. But there is evidence that food colorings, particularly red and yellow dyes, can worsen hyperactivity in a small percentage of children with that problem.

Celiac Disease

A common allergylike disorder in children is celiac disease, caused by a chronic adverse reaction to gluten, a protein in wheat, corn, and barley. Children with celiac disease are sickly, have chronic diarrhea, and fail to grow properly until all gluten-containing products are excluded from their diet—a major challenge for parents. The gluten-free diet must be continued for life.

In addition to such adverse but nonallergic reactions, it has been established that food allergy is a very real phenomenon. It is exactly the same kind of reaction that occurs in all other allergies: The immune system somehow reacts improperly to a food, producing IgE antibodies that start the well-known sequence leading to allergy symptoms. The extent of the problem is in doubt. Estimates of food allergy prevalence range from fewer than 1% to more than 7% in children. Whereas the incidence of food allergy generally decreases with age, it is possible for an adult to develop an allergy to a food that was not previously troublesome.

Chinese Restaurant Syndrome

Often, it is a tricky task to differentiate between an adverse food reaction that resembles allergy and a real allergic reaction. For example, the well-known "Chinese restaurant syndrome" has some of the symptoms of allergy but is an adverse nonallergic reaction. The symptoms reported by sufferers include anxiety, pressure in the chest, and uncomfortable flushing of the face. First reported about 20 years ago, Chinese restaurant syndrome has generally been regarded as an adverse reaction to MSG, or monosodium glutamate, used in large amounts by some Chinese chefs as a food enhancer. In the past few years, however, the issue has been put in doubt by two carefully controlled studies in which volunteers who said they suffered from

Chinese restaurant syndrome were given capsules, some of which contained MSG and some of which did not. The studies found no link between MSG ingestion and Chinese restaurant syndrome symptoms, suggesting that the syndrome may be purely psychological. However, there still are believers on both sides of the issue and the debate goes on.

DIFFICULTY OF DIAGNOSIS

Diagnosis of allergylike symptoms can be a problem even when the symptoms are clearly food related because of the variety of foods we eat and the variety of reactions they can cause that are often not truly allergic ones.

Two studies have found that the phenomenon called "Chinese restaurant syndrome"—once regarded as an adverse reaction to monosodium glutamate, a flavoring in some Chinese foods— may be purely psychological.

People who suffer allergic reactions after eating vegetables or fruit may be allergic not to the food itself but to sulfite, a compound used to keep vegetables and fruit looking fresh.

For example, milk is a major allergen, but it can also cause allergy-like symptoms, such as nausea and bloating, in people who lack the ability to digest lactose, the sugar found in milk. Lactose intolerance is not an allergy. It is best described as a kind of indigestion, quite different from the allergic reaction some people have to the proteins in milk. (Lactose intolerance is relatively uncommon in Caucasians but more widespread in Asians.) Tartrazine, yellow food dye #5, can trigger asthma symptoms and allergylike reactions in some people. Food poisoning caused by spoilage or contamination can cause symptoms that can be confused with an allergic reaction. So can some digestive diseases. The problem is compounded by the fact that allergy symptoms sometimes occur hours after a food is eaten, so that cause and effect may not be easy to establish.

Another complication is that allergic reactions may be caused by contaminants or compounds used to treat or preserve food. For example, some foods may contain residues of antibiotics, insecticides, or molds, all of which can act as allergens. One group of food preservatives that has come under intense scientific scrutiny is the sulfites, which are used to keep vegetables, fruits, and seafood looking fresh and are also found in some processed foods, baked goods, and wines.

(Sulfites are antioxidants that prevent browning and that interfere with the growth of some bacteria.) Some asthmatics suffer severe attacks when exposed to sulfites. There have also been a number of cases in which sulfites have been linked to death from anaphylactic shock. Use of sulfites has been reduced by the food industry and their presence is now noted on labels of wine, under a 1988 ruling of the Food and Drug Administration.

When doctors diagnose a food allergy, they usually start by looking for other signs of allergy proneness in the individual, such as a family history of allergy or an existing allergy such as hay fever. The doctor will also look for symptoms that occur repeatedly after a person eats a given food. If a suspected food is identified, the doctor may use the tests described in Chapter 2 to make a definitive diagnosis. Skin tests may be used to distinguish between a food allergy and a food intolerance. The RAST test may also be used to get additional evidence.

One common method of diagnosing a food allergy is the elimination challenge diet, in which the suspected food is first banned and then put back in the diet to see whether symptoms occur. To help decide which food or foods should be eliminated from the diet for the test, a patient may be asked to keep a food diary, tabulating the consumption of foods and the occurrence of allergic reactions.

The most accurate kind of test is a controlled challenge. It is often done in what is called a "blind" or "double-blind" fashion to eliminate psychological factors. In a blind challenge, the patient is given either an inactive substance, called a placebo, or a sample of a food, freeze-dried and in a capsule or mixed with something bland, such as tapioca pudding, without being told what the food is. Both the patient and an observer—usually a doctor or nurse—record symptoms of an allergic reaction. In a double-blind challenge, the patient gets both the suspected food or a placebo without either the doctor or the patient knowing which is being given. This eliminates the possibility that the reaction may be psychological rather than physical.

A challenge test is generally done first with a small amount of the suspect food; the dose is kept small to avoid the risk of a severe reaction. If no symptoms occur, the test may be repeated with a larger dose. Several rounds of testing are often needed to examine the effects of all suspect foods. Once a food is identified as an allergen, the treatment is simple and direct: It is removed from the diet. The only effective treatment for a food allergy is avoidance.

Milk allergy is among the most common food allergies. Its sufferers cannot consume milk in any form and often have trouble ingesting cheese, butter, and ice cream.

COMMON OFFENDERS

A complete list of foods known to cause allergies would go on for pages, but there is a short list of common offenders. It includes nuts, chocolate, strawberries, eggs, milk, wheat, and corn. The list differs from country to country, because the amount of exposure often determines whether allergy develops. Milk allergy (as opposed to lactose intolerance) is more common in the United States, fish or rice allergy in Japan.

Unhappily, an allergy to one of these foods may rule out a whole class of products from the diet. For example, someone who is allergic to milk cannot consume it in any of its forms (whole, skim, condensed, dried) and may not be able to ingest such milk products as ice cream, yogurt, butter, cheese, and sour cream. A person with this allergy would also need to be cautious about a wide variety of foods that may contain milk or milk products: milk chocolate, puddings, cream pies, sauces—milk is even used as a binder in some brands of hot dogs.

The same is true of an allergy to eggs, which is less common than milk allergy but often more severe, raising the threat of anaphylaxis.

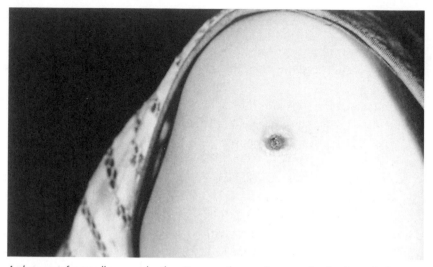

A close-up of a smallpox vaccination. Because the smallpox vaccination is made from a virus grown in an egg, some people who are allergic to eggs cannot be vaccinated.

Eggs are used in such products as waffles, pastries, ice cream, salad dressing, sausage, noodles, and mayonnaise. Egg white is used in the preparation of candy and pies. Routine childhood vaccination for measles, mumps, and German measles, administered in the first few years of life, can be dangerous because the vaccines are made from viruses grown in eggs. By 1977, worldwide vaccinations had virtually wiped out smallpox, and the vaccinations for this disease were therefore discontinued. Before this, some allergic people could not travel to countries where a smallpox vaccination was required because that vaccine was made in eggs.

Similarly, an allergy to wheat can rule out a whole range of products—obvious ones such as breads and cakes and less obvious ones such as malted milk, hot dogs, even canned soups and noodles, which may have wheat as an ingredient. An allergy to nuts or to a meat such as beef may rule out equally long lists of related foods.

MANAGING FOOD ALLERGIES

Organizations such as the National Academy of Allergy and Immunology, the American Dietetic Association, and the American Allergy Association have prepared lists of foods to be avoided when a specific food allergy is diagnosed. They also have listings of companies that manufacture prepared foods for restricted diets. Some of these products are available only in specialized stores, but many are sold in supermarkets.

Food-allergy cookbooks listing recipes that do not require such ingredients as milk, eggs, or wheat are also available. With a little ingenuity, it is possible for most people with food allergies to enjoy a fairly normal and tasty diet.

And although all the evidence is not in yet, allergists say steps taken by parents during the early months of life might help delay or prevent the appearance of allergy in children born into susceptible families. Nursing mothers are advised to avoid the foods to which their children might be allergic. They are told to breastfeed if possible because early use of cow's milk is suspected of increasing the risk of allergy. Some

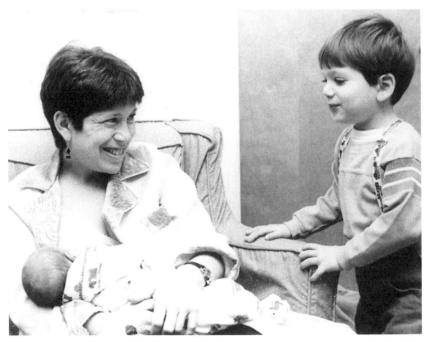

Some doctors hold that babies born into families who are susceptible to allergies should be breast-fed because drinking cow's milk at an early age may increase the risk of allergy.

doctors recommend that parents with a family history of allergy should not feed an infant any solid food until at least six months of age. There is reason to believe that the more scientists learn about food allergies, the more they will discover about how these conditions can be prevented and cured.

6

INSECT ALLERGIES

Beekeepers examine their collection.

What most people know best about allergies to insect stings is that you can die from them. Fortunately, however, deaths from insect stings are rare. It is estimated that over 2 million Americans are allergic to insect stings. Yet only about 40 people die in the United States every year because of allergic reactions to such stings. The toll would be even lower if current medical knowledge were fully employed—vigorous efforts are being made to reduce deaths caused by insect stings through a combination of better detection of susceptible persons, immunotherapy, and emergency treatment.

Almost all the insects whose venom can cause allergic reactions belong to a group called *Hymenoptera*, which includes bees, wasps, hornets, yellow jackets, fire ants, and harvester ants. They all inject their venom by stinging, not biting. The fire ant does bite, but only to grab hold of its victim; it then injects its venom through a stinger.

Most people who suffer an insect sting experience only localized pain and swelling. Those who are sensitive to insect venom can experience the usual range of allergic reactions. Sometimes they have only increased swelling and itching at the site of the sting, persisting for extra hours or days. In other cases, they can suffer symptoms that range from widespread hives and reddening and itching of the skin to stomachache, diarrhea, vomiting, a drippy or stuffy nose, shortness of breath, or aching and swelling of the joints.

It is important to recognize the first time that an allergic reaction has occurred after a sting, because the people who suffer serious allergic problems from insect stings are those who have been stung once before. An allergic reaction to an insect sting is a sign that the immune system has been sensitized—put on alert, so to speak—which means the next sting can bring a much more violent, even life-threatening reaction.

That sort of reaction is not inevitable. It is estimated that a person who has one allergic reaction to an insect sting has a 60% chance of another reaction if stung by the same type of insect within a few years. But a first reaction should be taken as a warning, because it has also been shown that sensitivity can last for many years. And although the severity of a second reaction usually can be predicted from the first—someone who merely has local swelling and itching is not likely to have a life-threatening reaction the second time around—immunotherapy usually is advised for people with known sensitivity.

COMMONSENSE PRECAUTIONS

As is true of every kind of allergy, the best defense against reactions to insect stings is avoidance. And because no one likes being stung by an insect, it is wise to learn enough about those that cause problems to be able to stay out of their way.

The bees most likely to inflict stings in the United States are honeybees, whose colonies live not only in commercial hives but also in wild habitats such as trees. A honeybee hive may contain more than 50,000 insects, most of them worker bees. These are females who cannot re-

Gardeners should be careful around their flower gardens, which can be a secret haven for insects. One important precaution is wearing shoes; another is wearing clothes that do not have flowery patterns.

produce and who do the foraging for pollen and nectar (incidentally performing a valuable service by pollinating plants). When a honeybee stings, it gives up its life. The stinger remains imbedded in the flesh of the victim and the bee suffers a fatal injury trying to tear itself away. By contrast, other species of bees and stinging *Hymenoptera* can sting once and live to sting again.

Wasps, hornets, and yellow jackets look somewhat alike. Wasps have black or brown tapered bodies with white or yellow stripes. Hornets have black bodies with white markings. Yellow jackets can be distinguished by the bands of yellow and black around their bodies. Each of these insects nests in different locations. Yellow jackets build large nests in the ground, often under stones, or on the ground—sometimes against the walls of buildings. Hornets build their gray or brown nests above the ground, on tree branches, houses, or walls. Wasps build smaller nests in the same kind of location, on trees or houses. Hornets are the most aggressive of the group, often stinging without provocation. Yellow jackets are close behind in aggressiveness, while wasps usually sting only if someone interferes with them near their nest. Fire ants, which are found in several southern states, have distinctive mounds.

A first rule for avoiding insect stings is to limit activities that attract insects. One sure attractant is food; yellow jackets are common visitors to garbage cans and picnic areas, and the other *Hymenoptera* are not far behind. Scents—perfumes, hair sprays, suntan lotions, cosmetics— also attract insects. Brightly colored clothes with flowery patterns do likewise. So the use of scented products should be strictly limited, and clothing with light, neutral colors should be chosen. Care should be taken with food outdoors. Even pet food left in a dish on a porch can attract stinging insects. In general, food outdoors should be covered as much as possible and spills should be cleaned up promptly. Garbage cans should be covered, and garbage areas should be as clean as possible.

Activities such as gardening that might bring about accidental encounters with stinging insects should be undertaken with great care. Even a barefoot walk across a lawn can be dangerous because the path might lie in the direction of a yellow jacket nest. Mowing the lawn can be hazardous for the same reason and should never be done barefoot. Any object on which an insect might alight—including children's toys, wagon handles, and gardening tools—should be checked before it is picked up.

Known insect nests and hives near the home of anyone with a known insect sting allergy should be removed or destroyed— by someone other than the allergic person. The exact technique depends on the kind of nest. The best time for attacking a yellow jacket nest is in the evening, when all of its inhabitants have returned from foraging. Gasoline, kerosene, or lye should be poured into the entrance opening, and the treatment should be repeated the following evening. (The gasoline or kerosene should not be lighted; the fumes alone will kill the insects.) A yellow jacket nest should never be hosed down, because the insects may be provoked to attack anyone nearby. A wasp nest can be knocked to the ground with a stick or stream of water. It should then immediately be placed into a tightly closed container. Another way to destroy a wasp nest is by hosing it down vigorously.

Hornet nests sometimes require professional attention, because they are often built high in a tree. A nest can be burned out or put into a sealed container and removed. A professional exterminator or fire department can handle hard-to-reach hornet nests. Beehives can be managed in the same way. If they contain honeybees, a local beekeeper may be pleased to add the hive to his or her collection.

ANAPHYLACTIC SHOCK

One August afternoon, while Phoebe was hiking with her friends, she was stung by a wasp. Phoebe grimaced, but informed her companions that they need not worry: She had been stung a couple of months before and had suffered no ill effects. "At least I'm not allergic," she said.

A few minutes later, however, Phoebe felt light-headed and needed to rest. As the minutes passed her symptoms got worse. Her head began to throb painfully, her skin itched, and she had trouble breathing. Her companions ran for help.

Phoebe was exhibiting symptoms of anaphylactic shock, a condition caused by her body's reaction to the wasp sting—not the sting she had just received but the one she had previously suffered. This delayed reaction typifies anaphylactic shock. It occurs only after the body has already been exposed to an irritant such as insect venom, a particular food (shellfish, for example), or a drug (often an antibiotic or antihistamine). After this first incident, the immune system creates antibodies as a preventive measure against future attacks. If and when the second episode occurs, the immune system recognizes the antigen, or harmful invader, and looses its arsenal of antibodies to counterattack. The result is anaphylactic shock.

The symptoms of anaphylactic shock are dangerous and can prove fatal. Phoebe experienced heart palpitations, a sudden drop in blood pressure, and the beginnings of respiratory distress. This last symptom is especially hazardous; in some cases, the victim's breathing may become so impaired that he or she requires oxygen or even an incision made in the trachea to allow an unobstructed pathway for air.

Victims of anaphylactic shock must be treated immediately with medication. Usually, epinephrine and cortisone derivatives reverse the internal actions, and antihistamines may relieve the patient's physical discomfort. But if the patient is allergic to antihistamines, these compounds can worsen the anaphylaxis.

Because anaphylactic shock is so unpredictable, it often cannot be prevented. There are safeguards, however, that can lessen the chances that the condition will occur. Doctors can test patients for allergic reactions by performing skin tests before administering antibiotics or other potential allergens. And people who have suffered severe reactions to insect stings can obtain emergency kits that contain the measures for treating the symptoms of anaphylactic shock—measures that can mean the difference between life and death.

The best way to destroy a hornet's nest is to set it afire or place it in a sealed can. The nests can be hard to reach, however, because they are often built high up in trees.

GETTING HELP

The first step in diagnosing an insect-sting allergy is for the doctor to make a careful record of the kind of reaction occurring after a sting. It is helpful if the patient can describe the species of insect that inflicted the sting. A definite diagnosis usually requires a skin test, using one of five commercially marketed venoms. A skin test can determine the presence or absence of an insect-sting allergy in all but 5% of cases. A RAST test may be done when the results of a skin test are inconclusive, although allergists caution that RAST tests and skin tests sometimes provide conflicting results about the presence and severity of the allergic reaction.

If an allergy is diagnosed, immunotherapy—allergy shots—is often recommended. Formerly, immunotherapy for insect stings consisted of injections of extracts from the whole bodies of the insect. Studies indicated, however, that extracts from venom alone were more effective, and these new extracts have been widely adopted. The same five commercial venoms used in skin tests— honeybee, wasp, yellow jacket, and two species of hornet—are used in immunotherapy. The treatment starts with weekly injections of a very small amount of venom, about a hundredth of a microgram, and continues while the amount is progressively increased to about 100 micrograms. The time between injections is then lengthened, until the patient gets one shot every four, six, or eight weeks. It is now recommended that patients continue immunotherapy for insect venom over the course of their lifetime. However, this recommendation is under study because it has been found that the protection still exists for many patients one or two years after immunotherapy is stopped. In those cases, the patients had been getting shots for a minimum of five years.

The effectiveness of injection therapy is checked by measuring levels of IgE and IgG antibodies to insect venom in the patient. Properly done, immunotherapy is believed to be highly effective and safe. One of every six patients suffers some reaction to the injections, but these generally happen early in the treatment and are mild. If the reaction is more severe, the doctor may reduce the dose of venom in the next injection, increasing it gradually later.

Because injection therapy is relatively expensive and goes on for so long, scientists are studying ways to determine in advance which patients

Anyone who has suffered an allergic reaction to an insect sting should wear a Medic Alert tag and carry a card that contains information about the allergy.

will benefit and which can do without the treatment. Long-term studies of both adults and children were started in 1987 under the auspices of the National Institutes of Health at Johns Hopkins Medical Institutions in Baltimore. In a study of children that enlisted 242 volunteers, it was found that immunotherapy reduced the incidence of allergic reactions to stings. But one unexpected finding was that the incidence of reactions in children who did not get injection therapy was lower than expected, in the neighborhood of 10%. The tentative conclusion was that a child whose first allergic reaction to an insect sting is mild, with skin symptoms only, may not need immunotherapy.

FIRST AID

Anyone known to be in danger of a severe reaction to an insect sting should always have an emergency first-aid kit on hand. The patient's doctor should demonstrate how the kit is used and have the patient practice its use. A kit will typically include a syringe containing epinephrine (Adrenalin), the leading drug for allergic reactions.

When someone with an insect allergy is stung, the first step that should be taken is removal of the stinger and venom sac if they are still on the skin, using tweezers, a knife, or even a fingernail. The venom sac should not be squeezed, lest more venom be injected. If it is available, ice should be applied to the site of the sting. If an arm or leg has been stung, a tourniquet, or tight bandage, should be applied above the site to slow the spread of the venom. It should be loosened briefly every 10 minutes.

The prepackaged epinephrine from an emergency kit should be injected under the skin, not into a blood vessel or muscle, at the first sign of an anaphylactic reaction. An antihistamine pill should be taken after the injection. Meanwhile, the patient should be rushed to a hospital emergency room or doctor's office and kept under observation for an hour or two even if the reaction appears to be under control.

Anyone who has experienced an allergic reaction to a sting should wear a Medic Alert identification tag or bracelet (available from the Medic Alert Foundation, Box 1009, Turlock, CA 95380) and should carry a card giving information about the nature of the allergy and treatment of a reaction.

7

DRUG ALLERGIES

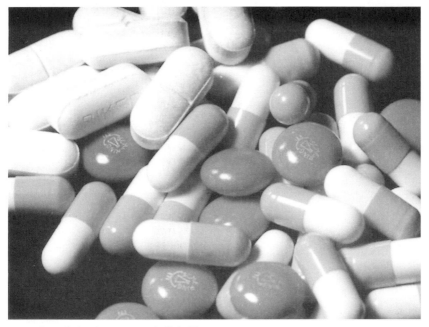

Drugs have helped many people fight illnesses.

We take medicine to do ourselves good—to prevent an illness, cure it, or lessen its symptoms. But every medicine has its risks. As medicines have become more numerous and powerful, the number of adverse side effects has grown. The federal Department of Health and Human Services estimates that adverse reactions to drugs are responsible for more than 10% of all hospital admissions, and that up to 30% of hospitalized patients suffer adverse reactions to drugs.

IDIOSYNCRATIC AND PSEUDOALLERGIC REACTIONS

Most adverse drug reactions are not allergic in nature. Some are caused by overdoses. Some are unwanted but nonallergic side effects of the drugs—for example, the drowsiness patients experience when they take most antihistamines. And there are a large number of what doctors call "idiosyncratic" reactions experienced by some patients but not others. Idiosyncratic reactions are believed to be due to individual differences in drug metabolism.

A further complication is the existence of so-called pseudoallergic reactions to some drugs. These have all the earmarks of allergic reactions, but laboratory studies do not find any indication that the immune system is involved. The most common pseudoallergic reaction is to aspirin. Typically, the patient is a middle-aged person with a history of allergy who has been taking aspirin for years with no problem but then develops such symptoms as rhinitis (an inflammation of the mucous membrane of the nose) and asthma.

One explanation of this aspirin reaction involves leukotrienes, one of the mediators, or molecules that cause allergy symptoms, mentioned in Chapter 1 (and which will be discussed again in the context of allergy research in Chapter 9). Recent research has shown that aspirin produces its pain-relieving and anti-inflammatory effects by blocking the activity of molecules called prostaglandins. In some people, that blockage is believed to open a metabolic pathway that increases leukotriene production without involving the cells of the immune system.

Other drugs that cause pseudoallergic reactions include dyes that are injected into blood vessels for X-ray examinations, anesthetics, and ampicillin, a penicillin-type antibiotic.

TRUE ALLERGIC REACTIONS

True allergic reactions to drugs do occur. They come in the broad range of symptoms to be expected from any kind of allergy, from skin rash to sudden death. Estimates vary, but it is believed that allergy accounts for 5% to 10% of adverse reactions to drugs.

Skin Reactions

Skin reactions are the most common allergic reaction to drugs. In fact, it is estimated that 15% of all visits to dermatologists are for treatment of adverse drug reactions. Rashes, hives, swelling, and blisters are among the most common symptoms, but drug allergy can also cause something called exfoliative dermatitis, in which large areas of the skin begin to peel. We will discuss skin reactions in greater detail in the next chapter.

Photosensitivity

Another kind of allergic reaction to medication is photosensitivity, or increased vulnerability to sunlight. Someone who has this kind of reaction suffers symptoms only when exposed to sunlight after taking a drug. A usual result is an angry rash that resembles a severe sunburn. Drugs that often cause photosensitivity include the tetracycline antibiotics, thiazide diuretics (which are given to promote loss of body fluid), sulfa drugs (given to combat certain infections), oral contraceptives, and griseofulvin, used to treat fungal infections.

Lung Disorders

Allergic reactions to drugs can also affect the lungs. We have already mentioned that aspirin can cause asthma outbreaks in some people.

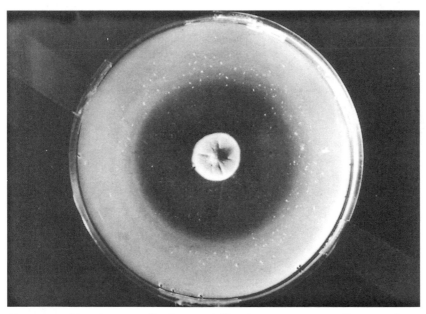

About 10% of Americans are allergic to penicillin. The symptoms generally appear days or weeks after the drug has been administered and clear up gradually.

Other drugs, notably the penicillins and sulfa drugs, can cause an allergic form of pneumonia. Allergy to some narcotics used as painkillers, such as methadone, can cause pulmonary edema, an abnormal collection of fluid in the lungs. A few drugs trigger an allergic reaction that causes inflammation of the pleura, the tissue that covers and lines the lungs. This reaction can be mistaken for systemic lupus erythematosus, a chronic disease that usually strikes young women. Symptoms of the allergic reaction will disappear when use of the drug is stopped, and lung damage is not permanent.

Other Disorders

Drug reactions can affect the liver, producing inflammation that is sometimes mistaken for hepatitis (an infection of the liver usually caused by a virus). A kidney condition called nephritis (inflammation of the kidney) is a symptom of some drug allergies. Drug allergies can sometimes affect the blood, causing hemolytic anemia (lowered quantity of hemoglobin caused by destruction of red blood cells) or destroying some infection fighting white blood cells.

A medical technician works on the preparation of an antibiotic. Allergic reactions to drugs can range from minor symptoms such as rashes and swelling, to dangerous liver ailments and anaphylactic shock.

Whole-Body Reactions

Some of the most frightening allergic reactions to drugs affect the whole body. One reaction is generalized lymphadenopathy, or swelling of the lymph glands throughout the body. The condition is not dangerous and disappears when drug treatment is stopped, but it can cause panic because it resembles the early signs of AIDS or cancer.

Another whole-body reaction is serum sickness, so called because it was first noticed as an allergic reaction to injection of animal-blood-serum products into humans. Serum sickness is now more commonly caused by drugs such as penicillin, sulfa drugs, and phenytoin, which is commonly used to prevent epileptic seizures. The symptoms of serum sickness generally appear days or weeks after the drug is given and clear up gradually as the drug disappears from the body. They include fever, hives, swollen lymph glands, and pain in the joints.

Fever

Fever alone can be another symptom of drug allergy. Fever caused by an allergic reaction starts a few days after the drug is administered and goes away quickly when the drug is stopped. Antibiotics and barbiturates are among the drugs that can cause allergic fever.

Angioedema

A potentially life-threatening allergic reaction to drugs is angioedema, giant hives that can affect the skin, mucous membranes such as the lining of the throat, and some internal organs. If angioedema occurs in the skin, it can be unpleasant and uncomfortable. If it occurs in the throat, it can block the breathing passages so that breathing becomes difficult or impossible. In some cases, emergency treatment is needed to keep a patient from choking to death.

Anaphylaxis

Anaphylaxis, the sudden, violent allergic reaction we described in detail in the previous chapter, can also occur in drug allergy. The reaction begins within minutes after the drug is given and must be treated quickly to prevent death. The treatment is the same as for an anaphylactic reaction to an insect sting: injected epinephrine and oral histamine, repeated as needed.

Anaphylaxis is not a common reaction in drug allergy, but it gets attention because it can be caused by some of the most widely used drugs, notably the penicillin antibiotics. Penicillin was the first antibiotic discovered, and although many others have come into use, the penicillin family remains one of the mainstays of medicine. Unfortunately, it is estimated that perhaps 1 of every 10 Americans is allergic to penicillin and that an allergic reaction occurs in 1 of every 50 persons given the antibiotic. Most of the reactions are not life endangering. About 75% cause skin symptoms, such as hives, rashes and contact dermatitis (swelling, itching, and reddening of the skin where it comes in contact with the drug). Another 20% or more of patients experience whole-body reactions such as serum sickness, drug fever, or angioedema. Roughly 2% of allergic reactions to penicillin result in anaphylactic shock.

The risk of a fatal reaction is one reason why doctors are told to perform a skin test every time they prescribe a penicillin antibiotic. Another reason is that penicillin allergy may not be permanent. About half the patients who have an allergic reaction to penicillin will have negative skin test results 5 years later and at least 75% will be negative 10 years later. So a skin test allows a doctor to prescribe penicillin for a patient who needs it. Penicillin itself is still used in medical practice, but doctors are more likely to prescribe one of a family of so-called semisynthetic penicillins such as ampicillin or amoxicillin, tailored in the laboratory to be more effective. (We mentioned that ampicillin can cause a pseudoallergic reaction; it can also cause a true allergic reaction.)

Another less widely used drug that can cause anaphylaxis is chymopapain, which is used to dissolve herniated disks in the spine as an alternative to surgery for people with chronic, painful back trouble. The risk of anaphylaxis from a chymopapain injection is estimated to be 10 times higher than that for penicillin treatment. Chymopapain treatment has fallen out of favor because of that risk. Doctors who use it are told first to perform both skin and RAST tests to rule out allergy.

Insulin can also cause allergic reactions, although rarely anaphylaxis. Until recently, diabetics used insulin extracted from pork or beef. Animal insulin is slightly different from the human molecule and so can cause an allergic reaction. Human insulin manufactured by genetic engineering is now widely used, reducing that risk. Some patients are allergic to the zinc used in most insulin preparations; zinc-free insulin is now available for them. Most patients experience only a rash or itching at the site where the insulin is injected.

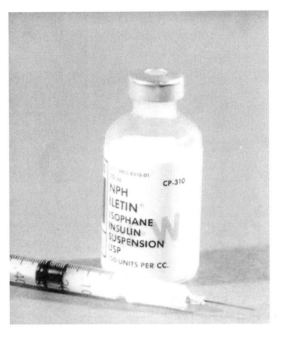

Scientists have been able to improve the preparation of insulin, which is used by diabetics to replace their own missing hormone, so that the medication contains fewer allergy-causing ingredients.

DIAGNOSIS AND TREATMENT

Drug allergies are usually diagnosed by observation. If the symptoms appear soon after a drug is given, the doctor can see if they stop when the drug is discontinued. The patient is often the key to diagnosing a drug allergy, since he or she is in the best position to notice symptoms and to know what drugs are being taken. Too many people make the diagnosis more difficult by failing to tell their doctor that they are taking over-the-counter products such as cough medicines, antacids and antihistamines; many people just do not think of these products as drugs.

Skin tests are not often done in drug allergy diagnosis, except for such widely used drugs as penicillin and insulin, because the drug itself may not produce any reaction when applied in a standard skin test. Often, the problem is caused by metabolites, the substances produced when the body breaks down the drug molecule. (These metabolites are chemically different from the "parent" substance and may cause allergic reactions in and of themselves.)

Treatment can be complicated by the need to keep giving a medication. The best treatment for any allergy is avoidance, but it is not easy for a patient with a serious infection to avoid an antibiotic or for a diabetic to avoid insulin. The doctor may have to make a clinical judgment, balancing the benefit of the drug against the risk of allergic reaction. Obviously, the severity of the allergic symptoms and of the illness are the important factors in making such a decision. Immunotherapy, or allergy shots, may be tried in some cases where use of a drug is important for a specific patient. Or if the reaction is relatively mild, antihistamines or steroids may be given along with the drug to help control symptoms.

Most of the time, however, a substitute can be found for the drug that is causing the problem—for example, acetaminophen instead of aspirin. Allergy-prone people can mount their own defense by being careful about taking drugs. It is common sense to avoid taking someone else's unused prescription drug, but it is also common sense to realize that many of the over-the-counter products in the medicine cabinet are in fact medicines: Nose drops, antihistamines, or cold tablets, for example, can cause allergic reactions in some people. Anyone with a tendency toward allergy should approach all medications with caution.

8

SKIN ALLERGIES

Poison ivy.

As we have said, skin symptoms are common in most kinds of allergy. This chapter will talk about some common skin allergies. Heading the list is a condition that affects between 1% and 3% of American children. Doctors call it atopic dermatitis.

ATOPIC DERMATITIS

More commonly known as eczema, atopic dermatitis can begin very early in childhood, in the first six months of life. It appears as an itchy rash, first on the cheeks and scalp, later in the area of the wrists, elbows, and knees. Sometimes it can spread to cover most of the body. Constant scratching and rubbing will cause the skin to become thicker, crusted, cracked, and easily infected. In most cases, eczema disappears by itself by the time the infant reaches age two or three. But it can persist or return. Some patients have it into their teens, others all their lives. Their skin becomes chronically thickened and harder to treat.

Eczema is still something of a mystery. Most cases clearly have an allergic connection, and many can be traced to a specific allergy—to a food, for example. About two-thirds of babies who develop eczema have family histories of allergy and most of them will go on to have allergic rhinitis or asthma later in life. Studies have shown that IgE, the allergy-related antibody, is involved in most cases of eczema. Yet there are cases in which the most careful studies fail to find any allergy. Researchers are trying to find hidden links to allergy in those cases.

But treatment of eczema is based on the belief that allergy is at the root of most cases. Treatment in the form of prevention sometimes starts at birth. Parents who have allergies are told to breast-feed if possible and to avoid feeding their baby foods that might cause an allergic reaction. If eczema does appear, the doctor will carefully inventory the baby's surroundings, looking for the presence of pets and other environmental factors that can trigger allergy. Skin tests, food challenges, and elimination diets may be used to identify a food allergy.

Meanwhile, parents are told to take a number of steps to ease the symptoms. Rough blankets and clothing should not be used or worn, because they irritate the skin. Large temperature changes and excessively dry air can worsen eczema, so the baby's room should be evenly heated and humidified. Ordinary soap can also worsen the ailment, so doctors usually recommend special bathing soaps, oils, or ointments. Antihistamines and steroid lotions or creams can be used to reduce itching and lessen scratching. And of course, any allergen directly linked to the condition should be avoided.

There is no cure for eczema. But as we have noted, the condition often goes away after a few years. If it becomes chronic and persists into adult life, doctors may use special drugs to peel away severely affected areas of the skin.

CONTACT DERMATITIS

Another common kind of skin allergy is contact dermatitis, a reaction in which the skin becomes inflamed when it comes in contact with a substance. Contact allergy can happen on the job, for example when industrial workers handle such chemicals as nickel or chromates. Doctors and nurses can suffer contact dermatitis through constant handling of drugs such as penicillin. Other antibiotics, notably neomycin and streptomycin, can trigger skin reactions. A number of plastic and rubber products contain resins to which some people are allergic.

Cosmetics can cause contact dermatitis, although not nearly as often as the sellers of "hypoallergenic" products would have people believe. Some sunscreen products, perfumes, and lipsticks can be a problem, as can hair dyes containing a chemical called phenylenediamine. Eye makeup and nail polish are also known to cause dermatitis in some users.

Poison Ivy and Its Relatives

For most people, contact dermatitis is something that happens outdoors in the summer because of exposure to poison ivy and its relatives. Poison ivy is the best known of a group of plants that produce a sap containing an oily substance called urushiol. Poison oak and poison sumac produce almost identical forms of urushiol. It is a potent allergen that can remain active for more than a year. Up to 70% of Americans will develop contact dermatitis if exposed to large amounts of

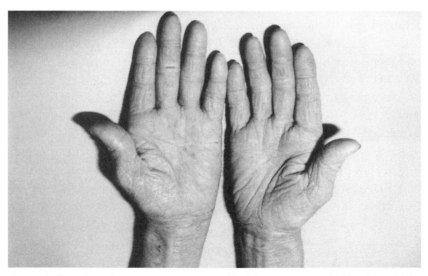

Experts believe that allergy causes eczema, a skin inflammation marked by dry and itchy skin. Although there is no direct cure for this condition it is often a temporary ailment that disappears by itself.

urushiol. For half of them, contact with even a small amount is enough to produce a rash, itching, pain, and blisters.

Just rubbing against a poison ivy, oak, or sumac plant can lead to an allergic reaction. But there are other ways to make contact with urushiol: by petting an animal that has rubbed against the plant, by handling a tool that has the sap on it, even by exposure to the smoke of a burning plant. However, you cannot get contact dermatitis by touching the skin of someone who has the condition, as long as all the urushiol-containing sap has been washed off.

This kind of contact dermatitis occurs in a two-step process in which cells rather than antibodies play the major role. The first time contact is made with poison ivy, oak, or sumac, nothing visible happens. But the urushiol seeps into the skin and sets the stage for a later reaction by first combining with proteins in the body and then sensitizing white blood cells. In some people, that process leads nowhere in particular; they will not suffer any symptoms on future contact. In other people, a second contact with urushiol causes the sensitized white cells to release mediators that produce the familiar, painful skin symptoms. And in others, a series of exposures may be needed to cause the reaction. The reason for the differences is a mystery. Although heredity helps explain why people develop allergic rhinitis, family history does not seem to have anything to do with poison ivy allergy. A further mystery is that individuals with eczema are less likely to react to urushiol, for no apparent reason.

It can take anywhere from four hours to several days after contact is made for poison ivy symptoms to appear; typically, they are evident in two to four days. The area of the skin that made contact becomes red, swollen, and itchy. Blisters appear, break, and ooze, until they start to crust over. The symptoms usually peak in five days, then gradually diminish until they disappear in a week or two. It is unusual for contact dermatitis to develop into a serious condition, but complications such as infections of the inflamed area can occur.

Those symptoms are not inevitable. If you know that contact has been made, vigorously washing the parts of the skin and clothing that touched the plant can get rid of the urushiol before the allergic process begins. The sap has to be washed off completely within five minutes to prevent all symptoms; even if this is not achieved, the more sap that is removed, the smaller the affected area will be. Plain water will do to wash off the sap. Soap helps, but rubbing alcohol will make things worse. Someone who has had severe symptoms in the past should see a

Contact dermatitis affects many men and women who work with chemicals such as chromates. The allergy can also be caused by cosmetics, sunscreen products, and hair dyes.

doctor at once. Oral steroids can prevent or alleviate symptoms if they are taken soon after exposure.

Once the symptoms start, the best thing to do is to ease the pain and itching. Not much about poison ivy treatment has changed over the years. Cold compresses, calamine lotion, and Burow's solution can help relieve pain and itching. A doctor may prescribe an antihistamine or a steroid lotion or cream in some cases. It is best to see a doctor if the rash covers a large portion of the body or reaches sensitive regions, such as the genitals or near the eyes. Oral steroids may be prescribed in very severe cases.

Other Plants

Poison ivy, oak, and sumac are not the only plants that can cause contact dermatitis. Ragweed sap can trigger it in some sensitive people. This sap contains sesquiterpine lactone, an allergen that is a member of a family of chemicals found in a number of other plants, including sagebrush, wormwood, and chrysanthemum. (The allergen in ragweed that causes contact dermatitis has nothing to do with the one that causes hay fever.) Still other plants can cause contact dermatitis. In Europe, primrose is the main culprit. In the American Southwest, the heliotrope plant can produce skin reactions in people who walk in the desert. Some people are allergic to common house and garden plants, including daisies and tulips.

TREATING SKIN ALLERGIES

Injection therapy for poison ivy, oak, and sumac allergies has not been very successful. These shots use increasing amounts of urushiol to induce tolerance. The problem is that injections that give enough urushiol to produce a benefit can cause severe reactions, both at the injection site and elsewhere in the body. However, better success has been reported with immunotherapy in which urushiol is given by mouth. Oral therapy can trigger local symptoms but reduces vulnerability if continued long enough. In 1987 an expert panel appointed by the Food and Drug Administration recommended not using injection therapy for poison ivy allergy but gave qualified approval to oral immunotherapy.

Of course, everyone should know enough about poison ivy to avoid "pretty little three-leaves," as it is sometimes called because its shiny leaves grow in groups of three. Poison ivy grows as a vine or shrub. When it loses its leaves, poison ivy can be identified by its greenish-white berries. Poison oak resembles poison ivy, except that the undersides of its leaves are much lighter than the tops and are covered with hair. Poison sumac is a small tree that grows in swampy areas. The best way to identify it is by its berries, which are green and hang in clusters. Harmless sumacs have red berries in upright clusters.

These plants should be avoided or destroyed. Burning is not recommended because the smoke can cause an allergic reaction. Herbicides such as ammonium sulfate, silvex, and amitrole can kill the plants, but they should be used with care and only as instructions recommend because they can be health hazards if mishandled.

As for other common skin allergies, we have already mentioned that reactions to foods, drugs, or other allergens can produce urticaria, or hives, which are patches of itching and swelling. (Urticaria can also occur inside the body, causing symptoms that range from breathing problems to headaches to stomach pain, depending on the site.) Some people have chronic hives that can be produced not only by allergens but also by emotional factors. Hives are treated by removing any known allergen and by giving histamines and steroids to lessen symptoms.

9

RESEARCH FRONTIERS

Histamine research.

Because so many Americans suffer from allergies, it is not surprising that the federal government, various universities, and pharmaceutical companies conduct a lot of research on the subject. For example, the National Institute of Allergy and Infectious Diseases not only sponsors research at its headquarters at Bethesda, Maryland, but has also established 12 centers for allergy and asthma research at universities and clinics around the country.

Much of that research is aimed directly at providing better care for people who have allergies. Some researchers are trying to develop better pollen extracts for hay fever immunotherapy. Others are working on better skin tests to diagnose drug and dust allergies. Still others are doing studies to predict if and when children will lose their allergy to a given food, in order to reduce the time they need be kept on limited diets.

The aim of this clinically oriented research is to produce benefits as fast as possible, generally by coming up with improvements in current techniques. Some of those benefits are already available (for instance, the more effective venom extracts for insect allergy shots discussed in Chapter 6), and others are almost ready for practical use.

UNLOCKING THE SECRETS
OF THE IMMUNE SYSTEM

Perhaps the most fascinating allergy research is work that aims at achieving a better basic understanding of the immune system and its disorders. It is fascinating because basic research ties allergy to most of the major unsolved problems in medicine today. A better understanding of immunology, the science of the immune system, is the key to allergy prevention and treatment. But it is also the key to AIDS, organ trans-

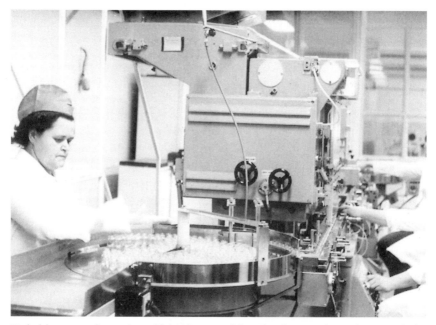

Technicians manufacture bronchial asthma medicine. The discovery that asthma attacks in two stages—one immediate and one delayed—has opened the way for better treatment.

plantation, and autoimmune diseases (in which the body attacks its own tissue), which include rheumatic fever and rheumatoid arthritis.

One way or another, the immune system affects just about everything in the human body, and vice versa. One of the more interesting areas of research today concerns the relationship between emotions and illness. There is strong evidence that grief and bereavement can make people more susceptible to sickness by weakening the immune system. A study done at Mount Sinai Medical Center in New York produced typical findings. Testing men whose wives died of breast cancer, the researchers found a reduction in T cell activity and other measures of immune system function. (It is not clear yet whether that reduced function will lead to illness.)

There is a link to allergy here; we know that emotional upsets and stressful conditions can worsen attacks of some allergies and of asthma. (The same thing can happen in rheumatoid arthritis and other autoimmune diseases.) A mental occurrence can produce a physical effect. Some researchers have found that chemical mediators, such as histamine, that cause allergy and asthma symptoms also make muscle cells in the airways to the lungs more sensitive to hormones released by nerves. So any emotional upset that increases nerve activity could aggravate an asthma attack. If scientists can find some way of interfering with that process, asthma sufferers will be helped.

MARSHALING THE BODY'S OWN CHEMICALS

Researchers are also exploring a number of chemical pathways in the body for the purpose of helping people with allergies and asthma. One particularly promising pathway starts with a common body chemical called arachidonic acid. Research has shown that arachidonic acid is the parent compound for several groups of powerful natural chemicals, all of which play important roles in health and sickness. One of these groups is the prostaglandins, which are involved in functions as varied as childbirth and inflammation. We now know that, in fact, aspirin fights pain and reduces inflammation by inhibiting the production of prostaglandins. (Like histamines and other mediators we discussed earlier, prostaglandins produce annoying symptoms in the process of performing necessary and helpful functions in the body. Scientists try to maximize their good effects and minimize the bad ones.)

Scientists conduct an AIDS test. A better understanding of the immune system is not only essential to the treatment and prevention of allergies but also may be the key to a future cure for AIDS.

By another pathway, arachidonic acid can be metabolized to produce the chemicals called leukotrienes, identified as playing an important role in allergy. Leukotrienes are supposed to be released by leukocytes (white blood cells) to help fight damage or disease. Leukotrienes are signal molecules that tell the body's cells to do things that are supposed to be helpful. Some cells are told to rush to the site of an injury, others to manufacture and release chemicals that attack harmful invaders. But in allergy and asthma the leukotriene response is inappropriate, and that causes trouble.

In allergic reactions, leukotrienes (like other mediators, such as histamine) are released when the immune system mistakenly identifies something as harmless as ragweed as a dangerous invader. What is believed to happen in asthma is that the leukotrienes mistakenly signal the muscles of the airways to contract. That contraction can be helpful in a noxious environment, because it cuts down the flow of contaminated air. In asthma. reduced airflow is unnecessary and harmful.

A drug that blocks leukotriene activity could thus be very helpful. But leukotrienes are complicated molecules, of which there are at least five types, each with a different function in the body. There is also uncertainty about the importance of leukotrienes compared to histamine and other mediators in allergy and asthma. The first trials of antileukotriene drugs developed by universities and pharmaceutical companies were disappointing. Researchers have since developed new drugs that have been approved and are being marketed. Although they were first approved for use in asthma patients, they may also have a role in treating allergic rhinitis.

To date the major success story is histamine, the discovery of which led not only to drugs for allergy and asthma but also to medication for ulcers. A less successful story is research on the prostaglandins, into which tens of millions of dollars were poured in hopes that they would be the miracle drugs of the 1980s. Most of the hope remains unfulfilled, although one or two prostaglandin products are in medical use. However, prostaglandin research goes on.

Another promising line of research takes off from the recent discovery that in asthma and allergy there are two allergic responses, separated in time. The early response is that described throughout this book: An allergen causes production of IgE, which binds to mast cells or basophils and makes them release histamine and other mediators. The second response occurs hours later. Cells of the immune system, mainly basophils and eosinophils, are attracted to the area where the early allergic response occurred—to the skin in the case of atopic dermatitis, to the nose in the case of allergic rhinitis, to the airways in the case of allergycaused asthma. What happens then is not completely understood, but it clearly differs from the early response in several ways.

Release of histamine and other symptom-causing mediators in the early response is directly related to the presence of an allergen. That is not so in the late response, which takes place even if the allergen is completely gone. And the late response also causes inflammation. Researchers at several centers have identified what they call HRF, or histamine-releasing factor, which seems to cause the release of mediators by basophils in the late response. Studies at Johns Hopkins University in Baltimore, Maryland, indicate that IgE is also involved, but a different kind of IgE than that which triggers the early response.

Exactly the same late response seems to happen in asthma, in which the late response also makes the airways more sensitive not only to allergens but also to any irritant, even cold air. That increased sensitivity makes subsequent asthma attacks more probable and more severe. It is now evident that one reason steroids are effective in allergy and asthma treatment is that they block the late response, at least partially.

Research into the late response has raised several possibilities for better treatment. One would be to develop a compound that blocked HRF activity, either by preventing its production or by rendering it inactive. To do that, researchers must learn more about HRF—or more accurately, about HRFs, since there seem to be several varieties of histamine-releasing factor. So far, researchers have learned that HRFs are all about the same size and seem to have the same general structure, but they have not yet fully described that structure.

Scientists are also looking at the specific type of IgE that seems to take part in the late response. It appears that only certain people—for example, those with asthma—produce this special kind of IgE. This line of research involves both T cells and B cells of the immune system because they are known to be responsible, either indirectly or directly, for IgE production. It is known that people who do not have allergies do not produce IgE. It appears that T and B cells are different in people who have allergies than in people who do not. Nonallergic people have few or no B cells that are capable of IgE production. They also have an abundant supply of T cells that can suppress IgE production. A better understanding of how immune system cells normally refrain from IgE production could lead to better therapy for allergic conditions.

Basic research in immunology has uncovered layer after layer of complexity in the marvelously intricate system that has evolved to defend the body from disease. Much is still unknown about the complicated interplay of immune cells and molecules, and about the disorders that occur when the system goes awry. But immunologists are confident that their work will ultimately allow them to prevent allergies entirely or to at least cure some of them.

APPENDIX

FOR MORE INFORMATION

The following state and national organizations can supply more information about allergies, asthma, and immunology.

Allergies

American Academy of Allergy and
    Immunology
611 E. Wells Street
Milwaukee, WI 53202
(412) 272-6071
www.aaai.org

Asthma and Allergy Foundation of
    America
2269 Chestnut Street
PMB 481
San Francisco, CA 94123
(415) 339-8880
www.aafanoca.org

American Association for Clinical
    Immunology and Allergy
311 Oakridge Ct.
Bellevue, NE 68005

American Board of Allergy and
    Immunology
510 Walnut Street, Suite 1710
Philadelphia, PA 19106-3699
(215) 592-9466
www.abai.org

American College of Allergists
(800) 842-7777
www.allergy.mcg.edu

Asthma and Allergy Foundation of
    America
1125 15th Street NW, Suite 502
Washington, DC 20005
(800) 7-ASTHMA
www.aafa.org

Joint Council of Allergy and
    Immunology
P.O. Box 520
Mt. Prospect, IL 60056
(312) 255-1024

National Institute of Allergy and
    Infectious Diseases
(NIAID/NIH)
9000 Rockville Pike
Building 31, Room 7A32
Bethesda, MD 20892
(301) 496-5717

Asthma

American Lung Association
National Headquarters
1740 Broadway
New York, NY 10019
(800) 586-4872
www.lungusa.org

Asthma Hotline
(800) 222-LUNG
(302) 398-1477 (Colorado)

Association for the Care of Asthma
Jefferson Medical College
1025 Walnut Street, Room 727
Philadelphia, PA 19107
(215) 955-8381

Asthmatic Children's Foundation of
    New York
P.O. Box 568
Spring Valley Road
Ossining, NY 10562
(914) 762-2437

National Foundation for Asthma/
Tucson Medical Center
P.O. Box 42195
Tucson, AZ 85733
(602) 323-6046

National Jewish Hospital/
National Asthma Center
3800 E. Colfax Avenue
Denver, CO 80206
(303) 398-1565

Immunology

American Association of Immunologists
9650 Rockville Pike
Bethesda, MD 20014
(301) 530-7178

American Society for Histocompatibility
and Immunogenetics
211 E. 43rd Street, Suite 301
New York, NY 10017
(212) 867-4193

International Society of Developmental
and Comparative Immunology
Dept. of Anatomy
School of Medicine
University of California
Los Angeles, CA 90024
(213) 825-9567

National Coalition on Immune System
Disorders
P.O. Box 40031
Washington, DC 20816

APPENDIX

FURTHER READING

Berland, Theodore. *Living With Your Allergies and Asthma*. New York: St. Martin's Press, 1983.

Cherniak, Reuben M., M.D., Louis Cherniak, M.D., and Arnold Naimark, M.D. *Respiration in Health and Disease*. Philadelphia: Saunders, 1972.

Cumming, Gordon. *Disorders of the Respiratory System*. Oxford: Blackwell Scientific Publications, 1980.

DeKornfeld, Thomas J., M.D. *Anatomy and Physiology for Respiratory Therapy*. Sarasota, FL: Glenn Educational Medical Services, 1976.

Haas, Francois. *The Essential Asthma Book*. New York: Scribners, 1987.

LaFavore, Michael. *Radon, the Invisible Threat*. Emmaus, PA: Rodale Press, 1987.

Luce, John M. *Intensive Respiratory Care*. Philadelphia: Saunders, 1984.

Petty, Thomas L., M.D., and Louise M. Nett, R.N. *Enjoying Life with Emphysema*. Philadelphia: Lee & Febiger, 1984.

Silverstein, Alvin. *Itch, Sniffle & Sneeze*. New York: Four Winds Press, 1978.

Slonim, N. Balfour, M.D., and Lyle H. Hamilton. *Respiratory Physiology*. St. Louis: Mosby, 1972.

Weibel, Ewald R. *The Pathway for Oxygen*. Cambridge, MA: Harvard University Press, 1984.

Weinstein, Allan, M.D. *Asthma*. New York: McGraw-Hill, 1987.

Young, Stuart H. *The Asthma Handbook: A Complete Guide for Patients and Their Families*. New York: Bantam, 1985.

APPENDIX

GLOSSARY

AIDS: An acquired defect caused by a virus that impairs the functioning of the immune system; destroys T-helper cells.

Allergic rhinitis: Medical name for hay fever and other pollen allergies.

Anaphylaxis: A violent, sometimes fatal allergic response that occurs only after prior contact with an allergen.

Angioedema: Potentially life-threatening allergic reaction to drugs indicated by giant hives that can affect the skin, mucous membranes, and some internal organs.

Antibody: One of several types of substances produced by the body to combat bacteria, viruses, or other foreign substances.

Antigen: A bacteria, virus, or other foreign substance that causes the body to form an antibody.

Asthma: A breathing disorder characterized by a tightness of the chest and labored breathing accompanied by gasping, wheezing, and coughing.

Autoimmune disease: A condition in which the immune system attacks the body's own tissues and cells, mistaking them for foreign substances.

B cells: Immune system cells that produce IgE.

Basophil: Type of white blood cell involved in IgE production of allergic reactions.

Beta-adrenergic agent or adrenergic agonist: Type of bronchodilator that acts on adrenergic receptors, helps control breathing, and is less likely to produce harmful side effects than other drugs.

Bronchodilator: Drug that expands the bronchi; used to treat asthma.

Corticosteroid: Synthetic version of hormones produced by the adrenal glands and hormones that stimulate the adrenal glands; the most powerful drug for the treatment of asthma and allergies, but can produce many side effects.

Celiac disease: Allergylike disorder in children caused by a chronic adverse reaction to gluten, a protein in wheat, corn, and barley.

Contact dermatitis: Common skin allergy characterized by inflamed skin; occurs when skin comes in contact with substances such as poison ivy and allergenic cosmetics.

Decongestant: A drug that alleviates congestion of mucous membranes.

Eczema: Skin condition beginning in childhood and possibly lasting through life that manifests itself as an itchy rash spreading from the cheeks and scalp to most of the body; most cases develop from an allergy.

Elimination challenge diet: Method of diagnosing a food allergy by eliminating and then reintroducing the suspected allergen into the diet in order to determine which symptoms occur.

Epinephrine: Adrenalin, the leading drug used to treat allergic reactions.

Generalized lymphadenopathy: Swelling of the lymph glands throughout the body.

Histamine: The most common mediator; a compound that causes allergic responses.

HRF: Histamine-releasing factor; an action that seems to cause the release of mediators by basophils in a delayed response even if the allergen has completely disappeared.

Hymenoptera: Group of insects including bees and wasps whose venom, injected through a stinger, can cause allergic reactions.

IgE: A type of immunoglobulin; produced by cells of the lining of the respiratory and intestinal tract; IgE is responsible for allergic reactions.

Immune system: The body's internal defense mechanism against foreign substances.

Immunoglobulins: Globular proteins produced by the immune system to act as antibodies.

Lymphocyte: The type of white blood cell that includes T cells and B cells.

Macrophage: A type of white blood cell that destroys invading cells by engulfing them.

Mast cell: Type of immune system cell found in tissues near small blood vessels.

Mediator: A substance that can cause symptoms of an allergic reaction.

Metabolites: The substance produced when the body breaks down a drug molecule.

Methacholine: Used to test for allergies, a close chemical relative of a substance known to trigger chemical spasms.

Mucosa: Tissue that lines the air passages in the bronchi that, in asthmatics, becomes easily inflamed.

Photosensitivity: Allergic reaction to medicine that causes increased sensitivity to light.

Pollen count: Convention used to indicate to allergy sufferers how much pollen is in the air on a given day.

Prostoglandins: Part of a group of arachidonic acids; involved in functions as varied as childbirth and inflammation.

RAST: Acronym for radioallergosorbent test; an allergy test in which a doctor will extract a patient's blood and then expose it to a radioactively tagged allergen.

Sequiterpine lactone: A member of a family of chemicals found in a number of plants, including sagebrush, wormwood, and chrysanthemum; this substance can cause contact dermatitis.

Serum sickness: A systematic allergic reaction caused by drugs such as penicillin, sulfa drugs, and phenytom, whose symptoms include fever, hives, swollen lymph glands, and joint pain; can occur days or weeks after the drug is given and disappears gradually as the drug leaves the body.

Status asthmaticus: Life-threatening attack possible for asthmatics who do not respond to conventional treatment.

Sulfites: Food preservatives that can cause asthma attacks.

Urushiol: Oily substance in sap of poison ivy, poison oak, and poison sumac that can cause contact dermatitis.

Wheal: Small circular area of itching, reddening, and swelling that is a sign of an allergic reaction and a positive reaction to a skin allergy test.

APPENDIX

INDEX

APPENDIX

PICTURE CREDITS

Edward Edelson, author of *Nutrition & the Brain* and *Drugs & the Brain* in Chelsea House's Encyclopedia of Psychoactive Drugs, is science editor of the *New York Daily News* and past presi-dent of the National Association of Science Writers. His other books include *The ABCs of Prescription Narcotics* and the textbook *Chemical Principles.* He has won awards for his writing from such groups as the American Heart Association, the American Cancer Society, the American Academy of Pediatrics, and the American Psychological Society.

C. Everett Koop, M.D., Sc.D., currently serves as chairman of the board of his own website, www.drkoop.com, and is the Elizabeth DeCamp McInerny professor at Dartmouth College, from which he graduated in 1937. Dr. Koop received his doctor of medicine degree from Cornell Medical College in 1941 and his doctor of science degree from the University of Pennsylvania in 1947. A pediatric surgeon of inter-national reputation, he was previously surgeon in chief of Children's Hospital of Philadelphia and professor of pediatric surgery and pediatrics at the University of Pennsylvania. A former U.S. Surgeon General, Dr. Koop was also the director of the Office of International Health. He has served as surgery editor of the *Journal of Clinical Pediatrics* and editor in chief of the *Journal of Pediatric Surgery.* In his more than 60 years of experience in health care, government, and industry, Dr. Koop has received numerous awards and honors, including 35 honorary degrees.